Running Your Own

MARKET
STALL

Running Your Own

MARKET

STALL

Dave J Hardwick

KOGAN
PAGE

First published in 1992
Reprinted in 1993

Apart from any fair dealing for the purposes of research or private study, or
criticism or review, as permitted under the Copyright, Designs and Patents
Act, 1988, this publication may only be reproduced, stored or transmitted, in
any form or by any means, with the prior permission in writing of the
publishers, or in the case of reprographic reproduction in accordance with
the terms of licences issued by the Copyright Licensing Agency. Enquiries
concerning reproduction outside those terms should be sent to the publishers
at the undermentioned address:

Kogan Page Limited
120 Pentonville Road,
London N1 9JN

© Dave J Hardwick 1992

British Library Cataloguing in Publication Data

A CIP record for this book is available from the British Library.

ISBN 0-7494-0758-1

Typeset by DP Photosetting, Aylesbury, Bucks
Printed and bound in Great Britain by Clays Ltd, St Ives plc

Contents

Acknowledgements   7

Introduction   9

1. Setting Up   13
What are you going to sell? 13; Money
matters 18; How do I get on a market? 19;
Sunday markets 22; Other events 23;
Transport 23; Buying stock 24; Buying a
stall 25; Scales and measuring tools 26;
Insurance 26

2. Up and Running   27

3. The Market Trader as Businessperson   31
Employing staff 36

4. Types of Market   39
Town market 39; Non-charter private
market 39; Market halls 40; Sunday markets
40; Car boot sales 41; Flea markets 45;
Shows 45; Seasonal and holiday markets 46;
Street trading 46

5. Markets and Mobile Catering   49
Catering vans and trailers 52

6. Market Operating   55
Sunday trading 57; Scotland 59;
Conclusion 59

7. Suppliers   61

8. The Law   65
Shops Act 1950 65; Sale of Goods Act 1979
67; Consumer Protection Act 1987 67;
Misrepresentation 68; Misleading bargain
offers 68; The market caterer 69;
Fire-fighting precautions 75; Health and
hygiene 75

9. Publicity and Advertising   77

Appendices   **83**
1. Useful Organisations 85
2. Publications 89
3. Some Private Operators 91

Index   **93**

Acknowledgements

I would like to thank Jenny Barratt for her encouragement and Marion Rhodes for her support and help in obtaining research material.

I should also like to express my gratitude to the Environmental Health and Markets Departments of Derby City Council and the Trading Standards Officer of Derbyshire County Council for supplying me with copies of the various leaflets and publications which have played a vital part in allowing me to write this book.

Dave J Hardwick

Introduction

When considering setting up a small business, unless you are a tradesperson with specialist skills, it is a certain bet that somewhere on your list of possibilities you will consider market trading as an option.

There are popular misconceptions that all market traders are fabulously wealthy people who have an easy source of income and that it is a calling anyone can follow. Certainly it is a profession which is open to anyone, regardless of qualifications and experience, but what is not so widely known is that there are a large number of people who set up as market traders and fail miserably at the first hurdle.

Because it is a high profile business, ordinary members of the public see only the easy part, when cash is flowing into the till, and it looks glamorous. This image is cultivated to an extent, although unintentionally, by the traders themselves who work hard to present an acceptable public image, so important when dealing face to face with members of the public.

The difference between market trading and the majority of other businesses is that success is more a result of hard work and long hours than of cash resources, and it is this that makes it such an attractive proposition to so many people starting off on their own for the first time.

This book will take you step by step through what you need to do to become a market trader. The actual capital requirements are relatively modest compared to, say, a small shop, but it is important that anyone thinking of setting up on his or her own is fully aware that, while it doesn't cost a fortune in cash terms to get things off the ground, in work terms they will need to invest far more effort, actual physical effort, and time if they are to become successful. There are no exceptions to this rule and you have to accept this from the outset. If you are prepared to do the work, though, you will certainly succeed.

If you aren't physically fit, if you can't get up in the

mornings, if you don't want to work 16-hour days, if you don't want to stand outside all day in cold, wet, windy weather, you may as well forget about becoming a market trader.

But if you don't mind any of these things and are prepared to work hard for good results, if you want to be one of the close-knit band of professionals, and if you are prepared to consider the long term instead of the immediate future, you can, and probably will, succeed and become a member of a special community.

So where do you start? This is not such a difficult question as it might seem; in fact, most people have the impression that setting up is considerably more complex than it actually is. Perhaps it is an over-simplification to say that all you need is your stall, stock and a space but there is very little else.

The popular image of the market trader as the street corner spiv has thankfully almost disappeared, but there are still those who regard it as a second-class business – quite unjustified, of course. Nothing could be further from the truth, and the most positive recent development is that the banks and other finance houses are at last recognising that the established market trader is just as secure and reliable as any other businessperson, and in many cases more so.

One of the greatest attractions to many budding traders is that they don't have the problems of finding and paying for the running of permanent premises; instead their 'premises', their stall, travels with them to where they know there is a possibility of doing some business. This is hard physical work but naturally a great deal less expensive, with none of the legal hassles and expenses that premises seem to attract.

This doesn't mean that the market trader doesn't have any legal constraints. The law applies just as much to him or her as it does to a shopkeeper or any other businessperson. Also, certain aspects of the law apply only to market traders. For that reason, in Chapter 8 we look in detail at the law as it applies specifically to the market trader, and at consumer law in general.

We shall also be looking at car boot sales and flea markets because these are a fast-growing sector of the trade which can provide a try-out before plunging into full-time market trading.

Another aspect of marketing trading to be considered is catering. There are special problems which apply to this trade and it is important that, if you are thinking of market catering, you should be fully aware of what you are letting yourself in for both in practical and legal terms.

Finally, and most important, it should be emphasised, and constantly remembered by the new trader, that market trading is not a game. It is not a way of making a 'fast buck'. It is not a short cut to riches. It is a business, a business which - with a lot of hard work and determination - can, and most probably will, be highly lucrative. It is not only a business which will provide a good living and security for the future, but also a business which will be your passport into the market community, the community of professionals which is undoubtedly one of the closest knit and most supportive of all trade groups.

Chapter 1

Setting Up

You have decided that you are interested in becoming a market trader. You have looked around your local market and seen all the shiny new vans, and the pound coins changing hands, and you think you want a piece of the action. Where do you start? What is the first step?

As with all businesses the first step, and an important one, is to conduct some market research. The kind of market research you need to do can be enjoyable because it involves visiting your local markets and looking around, talking to your family and friends and perhaps to the people at your local cash and carry.

All market research is done with one objective: to answer some question or other about the potential market for certain goods or services. Your own research is to answer your main question: 'Is market trading really what I want to do?'

If, having asked around, talked to other traders and read the trade newspapers, your original feelings are confirmed you have to answer more detailed questions before you take a single positive step.

The most important of these, and the question which will to a large extent determine whether or not you eventually succeed, is to ask yourself what goods you want to sell on your stall.

What are you going to sell?

This question needs and deserves detailed study on your part. Look around the markets in your area and see what is selling well. Then ask yourself if your own capital resources are capable of supporting that product. For example, you might feel inclined to sell gold jewellery, and you have noticed that most jewellers do very well. Okay, that's fine, but have you thought how much gold you will need to put on a good display on a stall some 10 feet long (at least). Did you notice that all your local gold stalls also buy gold? Do you have the knowledge to be able to do the same – and the capital to allow you to do so? Unless you are wealthy to start with, perhaps gold is not such a good idea after all.

There are many clothing stalls on the markets you've visited and they all seem to be doing well. Perhaps that's another possibility. Let's look at clothing stalls. To start with most of the clothing stalls are double stalls, if not even larger, and they have vast stocks. Again, can you afford that amount of stock? Can you afford to buy your stock in such quantities so as to gain from the bulk purchasing discounts that the warehouses offer?

I have deliberately chosen these two illustrations because for some reason they seem to be the first suggestions most people make and they are not as attractive as they seem at first.

By all means, if you have a lot of capital, and if you have a knowledge of the gold trade, go for it. It is a good business, it is profitable, but it is not a business to consider if you are just starting up with a limited amount of cash. The same applies to the clothing business and for the same reasons.

These two examples illustrate something else which you should be looking at. When considering your trade you should weigh up how much knowledge you already have of the commodity you want to sell. An angler with a good knowledge of tackle will do well because he is selling to other anglers and can talk to them on their own level. A dressmaker will do well selling dressmaking materials because she can talk to the people she is dealing with on an equal footing.

So where does this leave you if you have no specialist knowledge? Does it mean that you shouldn't even be thinking of trading? The simple answer to that question is 'yes'. But have you given yourself the credit you deserve? There are many everyday commodities that we all take for granted that could be potentially profitable.

What about packaged food? We all eat, and certainly anyone with a bit of common sense should be able to form a fair opinion of what is saleable. The local cash and carry warehouse will be happy to advise you if you feel that this might be an option. The same could be said of toiletries, and both ranges are relatively safe too because they are non-perishable. In both cases a stall will do well selling these goods if (a) the prices are competitive (market research again) and (b) there isn't too much competition on the particular market where you are working.

If the price is right and there isn't too much competition, there is little which can't be sold successfully on a market stall. My personal knowledge would allow me to make a list of several thousand trades ranging from food to car spares to toys, greetings cards, sweets and confectionery, hardware and household goods, haberdashery, and so on. The list is endless.

I know of one trader in the North East who has made a great deal of money and is still trading successfully after 20 years selling off-cuts of Formica and other laminates to do-it-yourself enthusiasts. Another trader in Bristol, who started in the early 1970s selling second-hand washing machine parts, has progressed through new vacuum cleaner parts and spares to a chain of five or six electrical shops in the same part of the country – and he still works the markets at the weekend.

It is often said in market circles that if the price is right virtually anything will sell, and my experience over the years doesn't lead me to contradict that statement.

So far we've talked about goods. But what can be said about goods can apply equally to services and, again, if what is on offer is competitive you can succeed equally well by, for example, cutting and supplying keys.

Most of you will have visited markets and seen the demonstrators at work. These are the guys who set up stall and demonstrate one specific item. It may be a miracle kitchen tool or a special kind of silver polish, but whatever it is the demonstration attracts a crowd and once the demonstration is over sales are made to the crowd.

This always looks slick and easy but, believe me, there is far more to it than the person in the crowd will ever realise. First, you must have an outgoing personality. For this reason you will often find out-of-work actors demonstrating. You do not just stand up and start talking. Without exception, the demonstrator works to a fixed script, just like an actor in a play. The script is prepared by the manufacturers of the goods on sale and they insist that it isn't varied – understandably, they don't want their product maligned or false claims made which could lead to a bad public image. Demonstrating isn't something you should consider until you have a great deal more experience of working the markets and responding to crowds.

Likewise with pitching. The pitcher is the guy who stands up, usually on the tail board or open side of his van, and conducts a type of mock auction. Normally he sells household goods but this can vary. Pitching is an art and before you even consider becoming a pitcher you should study the professionals and even work part time with one of them. It takes a special kind of person to be a good pitcher and it is unlikely that anyone just starting out on the markets will have the knowledge or personality to make a success of it.

The other main area of trade is catering and on the market this ranges from the hot dog stand to the well-equipped mobile catering unit selling everything from cups of tea to full meals. There are special difficulties here but these will be covered in Chapter 5. Catering can be an attractive and profitable means of entering the business. Sadly, many people have realised this and as a result whenever a new market is opened the market operator, whether he is in the private or local authority sector, will be overrun with applications for space from caterers. Almost without exception, out of fairness to other traders, the operator will limit the number of catering stands on his market.

Let's assume that you have done your research, decided on a commodity and are now looking for suppliers. Much will depend on what you decide to sell. If you decide on eggs, for example, you may know of a local farmer who will supply you on a wholesale basis. Always try to find your own individual supplier for goods; that will give you an edge over traders who all shop at the same wholesale warehouses. That isn't to criticise warehouses. If you decide to sell something like household goods and you have to use a wholesaler, you will find that generally wholesalers are helpful to the new trader because they can see a lot of future business. So cultivate your supplier; let him know you are open to advice. In Appendix 2 on page 89 you will find details of the main publications listing warehouses and other sources of supplies.

To summarise, you should be looking for a commodity about which you have at least a little knowledge, which will sell in your area, which you can buy at prices that allow you to make a reasonable margin of profit, which is not already being sold to saturation point on the markets you plan to work, and which you can afford to buy with the capital you have available for this particular venture.

If you have no specialist knowledge you should avoid perishable goods, or high value goods which will tie all your capital up unnecessarily by being left on your stall or in your store place. Stick to something simple which you know you can handle.

One good idea which I have seen work many times for the newcomer is the 50p or £1 stall. This is a stall which carries a range of goods from toys to small household items, car accessories etc, all of which sell at the same price. The amount of capital needed is reasonable and the hassle of giving out change and remembering prices is non-existent. A number of the warehouses specialising in supplying market traders have a range of goods available for this type of stall.

If you are in a position to start up in August or September, you could be doubly fortunate as you can sell seasonal goods which don't require a big capital outlay but which will usually give you a quick return on your investment. The cost of setting up a stall selling Christmas cards, wrappings and decorations etc can be as little as £300–£400 and if you are on the right site you will recoup that outlay in a matter of days. Thus, not only will you have a few profitable months in which to increase your capital but you will also have an ideal opportunity of getting the feel of the market scene.

There are a number of traders who deal only in seasonal lines, changing from spring and Easter goods to summer gardening and holiday items and then on to toys and Christmas ones; this idea may appeal to you. There are endless combinations you can choose from but you must make certain that your market operator is agreeable to you changing your lines with the seasons as it could represent a change of trade which he wouldn't normally allow.

There is another good trade where capital is recouped quickly and that is the fruit and vegetable stall. A word of warning, though. You must buy carefully. Any stock you have left at the end of the day is unlikely to be of any future use and will therefore represent a loss to be balanced against your day's profits. Another important point with fruit and vegetable stalls is to look carefully at the competition. Certainly on established markets it is likely that existing traders will have a strong base of loyal customers; it is a fact of market life that this type of stall attracts customer loyalty more than any other. If you are considering this type of operation you should telephone your local wholesaler, or preferably several wholesalers, and ask for advice. Recognising that you are a good long-term business prospect as far as his warehouse is concerned, it is in the wholesaler's interests as much as yours to give you good advice.

If you are proposing to sell fresh foods, such as fruit and vegetables or fish or flowers, you will have to buy your stock on a day-to-day basis and this will mean early morning trips to your local wholesale markets. To get the best quality produce for your stall you will need to be at the wholesale market as early as two or three o'clock in the morning.

Money matters

Once you have decided what commodity to sell you should be able to gauge approximately what your capital requirements will be. Ideally, you will already have some capital set aside – perhaps your redundancy money, or savings made over the years with the eventual intention of setting up in business on your own account. You may need to consider a loan to set yourself up. If this is the case, be warned. You will not find it easy to raise a business loan either from the banks or the business finance houses unless you have a high level of collateral. It would probably be better to try to decide on a commodity which allows you to start up with your existing capital resources.

There are a number of trusts for specific groups of the community such as the Prince's Trust (for under 25 year olds) which can, and will, help wherever possible. If you qualify within the terms under which it is usually granted (you have been unemployed for a certain period of time, and you can raise £1000 yourself) you could receive help under the Enterprise Allowance Scheme which pays you £40 per week for your first year. It is well worthwhile investigating if help would be available in your particular circumstances by contacting your local Jobcentre or Small Business Advisory Centre, both of which can be found by looking in your local telephone directory.

You may be taking over a family business and coming into market trading for the first time. You may already have the capital and resources to buy an existing business. In either case it is likely that you will have had experience of trading previously and you should use this book to supplement your knowledge. There is no substitute for experience and if you have worked even part time in markets already you will have a head start against anyone who hasn't.

How do I get on a market?

Before you even try to get yourself a place on a market you must again do some market research to find out where you want to sell your goods and if those goods are likely to move at that venue.

There are many types of market and it is unlikely that at the outset you will be able to fix yourself up in all the places you want to go.

The best and most secure markets as far as the aspiring professional trader is concerned are the town and city markets owned and controlled by the local authority, or owned by the local authority and run by a private operator on its behalf. They have the best sites, traditionally in the town or city centres, and are the focus of the shopping activity in the town. Set up under ancient charters (which will be discussed in Chapter 6), some have existed for hundreds of years and shoppers gravitate towards them.

The only problem is, of course, that spaces are usually limited at all good markets and you may have to go on a waiting list, sometimes for years, before you get a stall. Some market authorities also allow stall spaces to be sold by an existing trader to allow him to get back some goodwill on the business he has built up.

You will not get space on a local market on a regular basis as a newcomer unless the market is newly opened or it is not a good trading market.

All you can do is ensure that your name is placed on the waiting list and be patient. Some authorities work on a strict rotation basis, although a number make special allowances for anyone who wishes to introduce a completely new line to the market.

In the meantime, you can usually join the casual traders list. This list consists of traders who haven't got a regular stall on the market but are prepared to turn up on a speculative basis and queue. Once the regular traders have claimed their spaces, and they have to do so by a certain time, vacant spaces will be allocated to people waiting on the casual list. Some local authorities insist that people trade in their casual queue before they are considered for a regular stall allocation. You can find out more about this, and the various operational requirements of your local market, by telephoning or calling at your local council markets department.

So, if you can't get on to council markets quickly, what is the alternative?

There are, in fact, a number of alternatives and foremost among them is the private sector where new markets are opening all the time. Details of private markets are published in the weekly trade newspaper, *World's Fair*, in its *Market Trader* supplement (details in Appendix 2, see page 89).

First, you need to decide which days of the week you plan to work. There is no fixed ideal but certainly in the early days you should be prepared to work as many days as you possibly can, bearing in mind that you must also allocate at least one day a week for visiting warehouses etc and your buying and administration.

Having decided which days you want to work you should then find out, either from your own research or from *World's Fair*, which markets operate on those days. Take care to consider travelling distances. The trader who arrives home after a 60-mile journey at eight or nine o'clock at night and has to be up at five the next morning to travel 80 miles to his next site is not going to keep that kind of travelling up for long. Plan your run of markets carefully.

It is then simply a matter of contacting the various operators. You can obtain their telephone numbers from *World's Fair*, or from an annual publication, *The Markets Year Book* (details in Appendix 2, page 89). It is best to telephone; few private operators ask you to write and even fewer have the administrative back-up to handle a volume of letters.

When you telephone the market operator you will be asked which market you are interested in. You will be told whether or not there are vacancies; if there are not you can ask the operator if he has any other markets on the same day which *do* have vacant plots.

Assuming there are vacancies, you will be asked to specify what you wish to sell. It is important that you give a comprehensive answer because you will not be allowed to sell anything other than the goods which you have listed.

The penalties for selling other goods can be severe, even to the extent of being evicted from the market, so make sure you give full information. You can always discuss changes later with the market superintendent and obtain his consent.

Once you have given details and the operator is satisfied that the vacancy on his site will be suitable, he will ask you how much space you require. There are two ways in which space is allocated. If the stall is supplied by the market operator you will be restricted by the stall size. This is measured in frontage and single stalls are usually 10 feet long and, yes, measurements are still the old non-metric ones. Therefore, on a market where the stall is supplied you will be restricted by multiples of the stall length, ie 10, 20, 30 feet etc.

If the stall isn't supplied and you are expected to supply your own, you will be allocated space only. This space is also given in foot frontage and you can usually book any space over a certain minimum, usually 10 feet. You will be charged on a basis of a rent per foot. This varies from market to market but the operator will tell you the rate when you book space.

You will be told what time the market opens to admit traders and what time it starts trading. You decide what time you arrive but you should allow plenty of time to set up your stall and lay out your stock attractively before the public start arriving.

Most markets will not allow any vehicular movement on the site after the public opening time so it is important that you arrive in good time. If you don't arrive by the set times, your space will be allocated to a new trader from the casual list and you will have no recourse of any kind other than to accept a different space – assuming there are any left – or to turn round and go home, having lost your day's trading and wasted the expense of getting to the market.

Nowadays rents are rarely paid in advance, and if an operator does ask that you pay for your space when booking at any time before the day of the market, you should make a few enquiries of existing traders to ensure that everything is in order before parting with any cash. At best you will be losing interest on money that you pay in advance of a market to the operator, and at worst the market will never open, the operator will disappear and you will have lost your money. In any event, no trader has ever been turned away from a new market because he hasn't paid the due rent in advance of the market opening date.

Your rent will be collected in one of two ways. You will either be asked to pay the rent as you drive on to the market or the market superintendent or one of his staff will visit your stall during the day to collect what is owed. The latter is the most usual method of working, and certainly the one adopted by all the established leading market operation companies.

Sunday markets

These first spread in the early 1970s following the repeal of the Sunday Fairs Act which, while in operation, had prevented any fair or carnival-type event opening legally on Sundays.

Since the Act was repealed and markets started to spread there have been literally thousands of new markets opened, and almost as many closed again. We shall look at the whole subject of Sunday trading in Chapter 8. Some of the original markets are still open and operating success-fully and at the time of writing it looks as though, over the next couple of years, the legal situation will change to allow Sunday markets to open legally. Currently, there are Sunday markets operating in almost every part of the country and it would be fair to say that they provide a higher level of trading than any other day of the week.

If you are starting in the markets business you would be missing out on a great deal of trade and experience if you decided against working on Sundays.

Spaces are easier to obtain and business is usually very high volume. The procedure for getting on a Sunday market is exactly the same as getting on a private mid-week market: phone the operator and ask for all the necessary details. The exceptions to this, where you are not required to make any previous arrangements with the operator by telephone or any other way, are always advertised in *World's Fair*. Instead you are told in the advertisement to turn up at the site at a stated time when space will be allocated on a speculative basis. The problem with this is that you do not get a good balance of traders and consequently both traders and shoppers lose out.

None of the established operating companies uses this method.

There are a number of traditional Sunday markets where this does not apply, and where, frankly, you just cannot get a space. Of these the most famous are the Quayside Market in Newcastle upon Tyne and Petticoat Lane in east London.

The position in Scotland is also somewhat different. Scottish law permits Sunday trading and all market operators are registered with the local authority in the area in which they operate. The authorities are stringent with their checks on market operators and this gives an added protection to the trader. Markets open throughout Scotland, and if you live there, or within reasonable travelling distance, you should take advantage of what is on offer.

Other events

There will inevitably be times when you cannot find a space anywhere, especially in the early days. If this happens you should consider whether your commodities are suitable for selling at galas, carnivals and other outdoor shows. All provide opportunities for you to set up your stall and gain both business and experience when you would otherwise have a blank day. Details of such events can be found in the coming events columns of your local newspapers.

Some traders end up concentrating on just attending shows but I wouldn't advise anyone starting up to do so. First, you are strictly limited in the number of days in your trading season and have to find something else for seven months a year, and also the rents charged at the shows are well in excess of those charged for ordinary markets; £100 a day is not unheard of, and you need to take a lot of money through your till to meet this kind of charge.

Transport

You are now at the stage where you have done almost all the preparatory work and can start getting down to business, or spending, whichever way you prefer to look at it.

You will obviously need transport to get you, your stock and your stall to the various markets and there is a wide range available; what you spend depends, obviously, on your capital. If your resources are limited you can, by looking in your local newspapers or a motor advertising paper, find a good van for less than £500, but you can spend up to £20,000 or more. At the end of the day, a clean one-ton van will carry just the same goods whether it cost £1000 or £10,000. Whatever vehicle you buy, it is important that it is reliable. It must start early in the morning and get you to the market, day in and day out. The market superintendent won't be impressed if you turn up late every other market day because your van isn't working properly.

You may have stock which is easily transportable by car, but will the car also carry your stall? As with everything else, you have to weigh up your needs and make appropriate transport arrangements.

If you are at the start of a business career you would be well advised to buy the best vehicle you can afford for cash rather than committing yourself to a heavy financial loan burden. That is common sense and applies to anyone starting out on a business career, not just market traders.

Buying stock

Once you've obtained your transport your next purchase can be either your stall or your stock – it really doesn't matter which. Of course, if you have been brave enough to venture into selling perishable foods, you leave your stock purchase until the last possible moment.

Buying stock is important because if you don't buy right, you can't sell right, and the result is that you will spend all your time at the market watching customers spend their money at everyone else's stall while they ignore yours.

How can you ensure that you buy right? That's a difficult question to answer, and there is no set formula to ensure success. It is a matter of taking as much care as possible, taking advice, asking around and not diving into the first warehouse you visit.

There are a large number of wholesale warehouses in every part of the country supplying goods suitable for market traders, and you can find out where these are by using Yellow Pages or hoping they will advertise in your local papers, or by investing in one of the specialist papers for the trade which carry pages of advertisements for all kinds of warehouses in all kinds of areas. The *Markets Year Book* is an annual directory which includes a list of wholesalers and is a useful tool for the new traders; details are given in Appendix 2 (see page 89).

Of course, you might be going into a trade you already know and your existing knowledge of the trade and its suppliers will place you in an advantageous position over anyone starting blind.

Buying a stall

You are now almost ready to start trading. There is just one more major item of shopping – your stall.

There are two main types of stall, although construction and materials used may vary considerably and what you need is determined not by preference but by your particular trade.

Ordinary stalls

These are of two kinds, described as 'walk-through' or 'counter'. The counter stall is the most common type and is the one you will see in most council markets. It has a simple board counter and a top cover. The walk-through is as its name implies – a stall which allows you to walk inside, like a small marquee with only three sides. Rental charges for both are based on the footage of the front of the stall.

There are a number of experienced manufacturers of stalls and their accessories in various parts of the country and the trade press carries advertising for them. They are all sympathetic and helpful to the new trader and at least one Birmingham manufacturer advertises a beginner's pack which includes the stall and everything else needed to start.

A full kit to start will usually cost just over £100, but if you look in the business section of your local evening newspaper you can often find stalls for sale for £50 or £60.

Both types of stall are collapsible so they can easily be transported by car or small van. If you are a new trader, practise putting your stall up a couple of times before doing it for real.

Don't forget when buying your stall that you will also need sheets, the canvas or plastic covers which form the top and sides of the stall, and spring clips which attach the covers to the stall itself. Your first day may be bright and sunny but you will soon experience windy days on the markets and you will then see the need for clips.

Scales and measuring tools

If you are using scales you should buy them from an established manufacturer. Scales used on mobile sales units and stalls are specially made to withstand the bangs and knocks of transportation and handling, and an ordinary set of shop scales will *not* be suitable. The Trading Standards Department of your County Council has a legal obligation to carry out periodic checks on scales in use in all trade situations including market stalls. Not only are you committing an offence in having inadequate scales on your stall but you commit a fresh offence each time they are used. You must not cut corners when buying, or leasing, scales.

The same applies if you are using any form of measurement; for example, yardsticks to measure materials. An ordinary three-foot rule is not suitable. Your measuring tool must be of a type approved by the Trading Standards Department and endorsed accordingly. Wholesale suppliers of materials etc will supply the proper measure and will advise you about this aspect of your business.

Insurance

There is one other item which should be mentioned at this stage – insurance. It is unlikely that on a private market you will be required to show proof of insurance cover for public liability, but most councils now require a copy of your certificate before you are allowed to trade on their site.

It is in your interests to obtain public liability insurance. It isn't expensive and it is comforting to know that if the bar at the top of your stall is blown off by a gust of wind and seriously injures a member of the public, you have insurance cover to protect you against the subsequent claims. Insurance companies advertise in the trade press and the trade organisation which represents market traders, the National Market Traders' Federation (see page 85), can advise you about insurance and offer a good premium rate through an associated insurance company.

Chapter 2

Up and Running

The big day has come and having been up before the crack of dawn you are on your way to your first market day. You did, of course, check last thing yesterday that you had everything you need!

Before you set out for market make a checklist of what you need to take, including such things as bags and wrapping, price tickets, a receptacle for your cash, scales for weighing if necessary. It is unlikely that you will remember everything in the early days but you'll soon be at the stage where you can remember all you need by habit. There is no better way of learning not to forget your Thermos flask than to have to go without a hot drink on a freezing February day.

The procedure when you reach your market will be much the same whether you are in the private or public sector. On arrival at the site you must report to the market superintendent or someone acting for him. You will then be allocated a space. You should enquire if this is to be your permanent space or if you are likely to be moving around for a few weeks until a regular spot is available.

You may also be required to pay your rent on admission to the site but that is something you will have been told when you spoke to the operator and booked your stand.

You should arrive in plenty of time to get your stall set up and your stock displayed attractively before the public start to arrive and spend their money.

There are two points to remember when setting your stall out.

1. Always show prices on goods either individually or clearly on signs around the stall. The majority of shoppers feel embarrassed about asking prices and may go elsewhere. Everyone you lose in such a way is a lost sale. The type and style of pricing are a matter of personal preference but prices should be clear and easily understood. Day-Glo card and tickets are useful

here and you can buy it in ready-cut ticket sizes at any
large stationery store.

2. You must, for your own protection, be careful not to
   make any claims about your goods which are false,
   exaggerated or misleading. We shall be looking at
   consumer law in Chapter 8 (see pages 67-68) but
   suffice it to say now that not only could a lack of
   attention to this particular aspect of your work be
   expensive in terms of fines and lost business, in
   extreme cases it could lead to criminal prosecutions
   and the loss of your business. You cannot be too
   careful. It is far more sensible to stick to prices only.
   Be careful to avoid claiming that the price is a special
   sale price unless the criterion for making such a claim
   has been met, ie the goods have been offered at the
   higher price at some stage in the previous 28 days.

Back to setting up your stall. Try to set your goods out so
that, while they look attractive and are easy for you to get
at when serving, they are not easily to hand for the casual
thief. It is a sad thing to say but petty theft is now a major
problem and constantly on the increase; you must protect
yourself against being a victim. Unlike a shopkeeper you
don't have the physical restraints of a door and walls and it
is easy for someone, especially in a crowded market, to grab
something from the front of your stall totally unnoticed by
you or, even if you do notice, to melt away into the crowd
before you can do anything about it. As a rule of thumb,
wherever possible you should always keep the most expensive items away from the front of the stall.

It may seem like jumping the gun a little but you should
remember when setting up your stall that you will probably
have to load most of what you are displaying back into your
van at the end of the day. If you bear this in mind it will help
you to keep some kind of order.

As far as pricing your stock is concerned, you will have to
play things by ear. You will already know the wholesale cost
of your goods. If you have sought the advice of your
wholesaler you will know what margin you should be
adding. You then need to research your competition and it
may be necessary to drop your prices slightly in line with
what others are charging for the particular commodity you
are selling.

Margins vary greatly, each type of product having its own

level of profitability. As a general rule it is usually the case that non-food items attract a higher margin than food. This does not apply to catering, though, where margins are among some of the highest earned.

You must also remember to manage your stock carefully, ensuring that the oldest stock is offered for sale first. This is particularly important where you are dealing in perishable goods. If you have only your van and stall this should be straightforward but it will be a little more complicated if you store your stock in a small garage or shed. You should set up a system from the beginning and stick to it. Not only does this allow you to sell your stock in order of age but it also gives you a clear picture of what is selling and what isn't, which is important information for you when you are buying.

Local authorities will, without exception, require you to display your name and either your home or business address 'prominently' on your stall. The term 'prominently' is open to various interpretations but usually means on a small notice board. This requirement is usually absent on markets run by private operators, but you should take special note that, where the goods you are offering for sale are covered by the Food Act, you are required *by law* to display your name and address.

A word or two about cash handling may be appropriate here. Remember that you are running a business and will be required at some point to account to the Inland Revenue. It is therefore important that you approach cash handling in a businesslike manner. You must have somewhere separate and convenient to hold your takings. This could be a cash tin on your stall or the more suitable apron-type cash pocket that most market traders use. These are reasonably priced and can be bought from the same people who supply your stall. They are certainly the best option as you have the security of having the money on your person and don't have to keep going back to your cash tin every couple of minutes for change.

You must always keep any personal cash you may have on you separate from the takings from your stall and you should keep a note of everything you spend in the course of your business, together if possible with a receipt.

So, at last you are ready to start taking money. How quickly and successfully you start trading will depend to a large degree on the quality of your market research.

Whatever your level of trading, you should not be disheartened. It takes time for your customers to get to know you and it is unlikely that you will make a fortune on the markets on your first day.

Market traders are a helpful bunch of people and it won't be long before you are accepted and part of the 'family'. Even on your first day you will probably be asked to keep your eye on someone else's stall while they are away for a few minutes. Alternatively, your neighbouring traders will offer to watch your stall when you have to take a break. That's the way things work and you will quickly realise that to a large extent a market is one large co-operative, a set-up which works to everyone's advantage.

Standing on your stall and trading can be daunting but it is largely a matter of common sense. You should be outgoing and as helpful as possible. The old adage that the customer is always right applies just as much to the market as it does to the shop, and you must always let the customer think that he or she is right even if you know that this is not so. Don't push too hard until you have found your feet and, unless you are a pitcher, which has to be agreed with the operator before you start, you should not be a noisy trader. Not only will you put your customers off but you will also annoy neighbouring traders.

Some companies and operators have rules about leaving a market before a certain time and they rightly enforce that rule. Nothing puts customers off more than a market with empty stalls dotted throughout. If you are one of the fortunate traders who sells out before the closing time of the market, frustrating as it may be, try to stay at your stall, or offer it to your neighbour to prevent ugly gaps. And if you have an empty stall next to you by mid morning, offer to extend your stock into that space. Provided that your market superintendent isn't a narrow-minded money grabber who tries to make you pay for the extra space, the whole market will benefit from seeing the space filled.

Chapter 3
The Market Trader as Businessperson

Only in recent years has the market trader's status as a businessperson reached anything like a realistic level. The simple fact of the matter, though, is that you have set up a business and you are now a self-employed businessperson with all the regulations and restrictions that any other businessperson has to comply with.

The most important aspect of any successful business is financial control and this is nowhere more applicable than to the market trader who, dealing with sometimes substantial amounts of cash, can be tempted into fast living and heavy spending; indeed, such is the nature of the market trader that he or she does tend to work hard and play hard.

As a beginner, though, you have to exercise restraint and plough all your profits, except your basic living expenses, back into your business. Build up your stock levels, have a bank account with some reserve cash. Once you are established on the market as a bona fide trader you will be offered all types of deal and you will need cash to take advantage of them. Also, if you do feel that you want to expand and you have been paying regularly into a bank or building society account, your request for a loan will be considered far more sympathetically if you have already established the fact that your business is sound.

We now come to an area which tends to worry some people, and that is bookkeeping, accounts, taxation and value added tax (VAT).

The worst thing you can do is ignore these matters and throw all your paperwork away or put it into an old box to be sorted out at some time in the future. That time never comes! The reality is that all these areas are relatively straightforward and only take a little time once a simple system has been set up.

For the purposes of this book a detailed analysis of all the requirements would be inappropriate. In any event many will depend on which aspects of market trading you intend to pursue.

The first thing you should do is find a good, *small*, local firm of accountants. Your bank or a personal recommendation from someone already in business are the best sources. Local press advertising or Yellow Pages can be useful but do not guarantee the quality of the service you will receive.

You should arrange to see your accountant briefly so that he or she can explain what records you will have to keep. You can also ask any questions which concern you. This meeting will not take long and could save you a great deal of money in the future. The format of your books should be agreed with the accountant and this will save you money when your accounts are prepared each year for the Inland Revenue.

Legally you will trade as a limited company, a sole trader or a partnership. It is unlikely that you will wish to be a limited company and for the purposes of this text we shall assume that you are either a sole trader or a partnership. You may want to use a business name. There are few restrictions apart from certain words such as International, Royal, Crown etc, which would anyway be inappropriate for your business. Details of the restrictions will be sent to you when you apply to the Registrar of Business Names to register your name.

VAT is an area that you will probably not need to concern yourself with initially. You do not need to register for VAT unless your annual sales are in excess of a set amount which at the time of writing (1992) is £36,600 per year. This threshold is changed from time to time by the government in its Budget legislation. Also, certain items are currently exempt from or zero-rated for VAT. These include fresh food and children's clothes at the moment but again, the list of items sometimes changes as a result of the budget. There are special schemes for retailers, including market traders, which set out the formulae for working out your VAT liability. Your accountant will advise you if he thinks you should be registered, or if you think you should be you can seek his advice or contact your local VAT office.

If you are not registered for VAT you must not charge any VAT on your sales and your bookkeeping will also be much more straightforward. You must, however, register for VAT

as soon as your sales get anywhere near the threshold unless your sales are exempt.

'Why should I keep records?', you may ask. There are a number of reasons: your bank manager may want to know how you are doing; you will save money in accountant's fees because his or her job will be easier (it may be an impossible task if you haven't kept records). You could also save a lot of money in taxes. For example, if you don't carefully record all your wastage you will not only be depriving yourself of tax allowances but you will also create large gaps in the credibility of your records. (If you are registered for VAT you *must* keep records.) You will also be able to monitor how well your business is doing at any particular time. It is almost impossible to keep figures in your head. Also, if the Inland Revenue query the tax calculations your accountant submits on your behalf, you need to have the records to prove his figures.

What then do you need to do? First, if you are going to have to write cheques and use a bank account it will be more straightforward if you open a separate business account. The records you keep will only be as accurate as the information you retain. You must therefore keep in files all your purchase invoices, cash receipts (for petrol etc) and a note of any items you spend money on for which you do not obtain a receipt.

The main areas in which you will be spending money are stock purchases, site rent, vehicle expenses, equipment purchases, insurances, professional fees and wages. Your takings will normally be in cash.

Certain household expenses may in whole or in part be charged for tax purposes to your business. An example is your telephone bill. You should agree this with your accountant. You may also be able to pay your spouse a wage (up to certain limits) free of tax and National Insurance for help on your stall or for writing up your books.

A separate book must be kept showing the daily takings from your stall. If you are not registered for VAT all you need to show is the date and the amount taken. Remember to adjust the cash at the end of the day to take account of any float you took with you at the beginning of business plus any cash paid out (eg site rent).

If you are registered for VAT you may need to keep separate figures for some of your takings that are either zero-rated or exempt.

Each week or month you should write up a cash book of your payments from the paperwork you have kept in your files and, if applicable, your cheque stubs and bank statements.

The cash book needs to have various headings. Here is a suggested format:

Date: Description: Cheque No.:   Amount:
Stock: Rent: Wages: Own wages: Other:

If you have paid by cash rather than by cheque write 'cash' in the cheque number column. All items should have the total in the amount column and also the column to which the payment relates, eg Stock. If you are registered for VAT the principle is similar but more detail is required for each transaction.

Ready printed account books are available with the headings laid out on the page and these make the job much simpler. If you decide to use one of these books you should take care to buy the right one. Different versions are available for businesses which are VAT registered and those which are not.

Finally, the dreaded tax bill. Your accountant will agree this from the accounts he prepares for you every year. The best year ending for a sole trader or a partnership is 6 April or 30 April if you use a month end rather than a week end for your bookkeeping. This gives you a tax advantage over people with other dates in that your tax is not payable for longer after your year end.

Your tax bill is based on the profit you make. Your profit, surprisingly, does not include any adjustment for the wages you draw personally. Therefore, if your accounts show a profit of £10,000 your tax bill will be the same whether you have paid yourself £5000, £10,000 or even £15,000 in that year. If you are not employed elsewhere you will be allowed a personal allowance, which varies from year to year, against your profits plus some other allowances if applicable. These may include mortgage interest relief on your house and a married person's allowance. The current tax rate is then applied to your profit, less allowances for the year, to give you your tax bill.

For example, your tax bill may be worked out as follows:

Profit £10,000 less allowances £4000 = £6000 × tax rate of 25% = £1500 tax payable.

Although this section has been kept as straightforward as possible, in reality it is complicated and I strongly advise all traders to have an accountant to work out their tax bills. An accountant will invariably save you more money than you pay in fees in the long run.

As well as tax you will be liable to self-employed National Insurance contributions. Your accountant or local Department of Social Security office will be able to advise you of the current rates. Usually they are based on a flat rate a week plus a percentage charge on your profits payable with your tax bill.

You may read this section and decide not to bother with all these complications. I can assure you that you will regret such a decision. You will end up with numerous problems and expenses which could haunt you for years.

Remember to find a good accountant, take his advice and keep all your receipts safe. A receipt for £10 saves you £2.50 in tax (at current rates). Those £10s add up over the year. If you have paid cash and either lost or not obtained a receipt, the opportunity to claim your expenses is lost for ever.

Clearly, the type of bank account you choose is a personal matter but if you are a trader whose business is almost all done in cash you would be well advised to look at an interest-bearing account, either with a bank or a building society. Why should your money earn interest for the bank and not for you? You will need instant access to your cash but that is really all, so why pay a charge every time you write a cheque? Many bank and building society deposit accounts now have a facility by which you can pay standing orders through the account so there is no reason why you shouldn't use such an account.

The Halifax Building Society's Cardcash or Maxim accounts seem ideal to me – the Cardcash if you don't need a cheque book facility and the Maxim if you do. These accounts allow you to draw up to £500 in any one day without any prior notice, provided you have that amount in your account, of course. This cash is available in virtually every town in the country which is particularly useful to someone who trades in towns which may be some 50, 60 or more miles apart. Most building societies offer similar accounts so it is worth asking around.

Employing staff

Initially, it is unlikely that you will be employing staff but if you do you should remember that the same employment legislation applies to you as to any other business. No one can have visited a market and failed to notice that a lot of casual staff are employed, particularly at loading and unloading times. This is perfectly legal, although it has to be said that corners are cut, and while not advocating wholesale breaches of the employment law, if you want to give someone a few pounds for helping you unload your van no one is going to make a song and dance about it. If you do so, though, you must remember that the money should come out of your pocket and not out of the business. Any money taken out of the business to pay casual staff must be declared in your accounts and any payments over £25 per year must be declared to the Inland Revenue. Your accountant will advise you on actual legislation.

A serious word of warning as far as employing casual labour is concerned: do so with caution. You won't be able to give casual staff any formal legal insurance protection, and if anything were to happen you would be responsible, as an individual, for any damages. You must bear this in mind at all times.

Public liability insurance has already been mentioned (see page 26). There is another form of insurance which is a legal requirement if you are employing people: employee liability insurance. Anyone in any business who employs another person or persons in the course of that business is required to take out an employee liability policy. This is not always straightforward as far as the market trader is concerned because to obtain cover under this type of policy you need to have business premises or, as the actual wording goes, 'a principal place of business'. The difficulty is that your business is run from a stall on a space at various markets and, as far as the insurance companies are concerned, that is not acceptable as a principal place of business. However, there are several ways round this problem and cover is obtainable legally and properly. Your accountant or insurance broker will advise you about this.

You could also, if you are a member, seek advice from the National Market Traders' Federation (see page 85).

Chapter 4
Types of Market

We have already learned that there are basically two types of market; those in the private sector and those in the public sector. That over-simplifies matters somewhat, though, and this chapter deals with the different kinds of market or market-type outlet.

Town market

This is the traditional market held in most towns and small villages on designated days (market days) each week. The majority are run and operated by the local authorities under ancient charter rights, some granted as far back as the thirteenth century. There is an increasing trend, particularly in the south of England, for the local authority to contract out the running of the market to an operating company. These markets are usually secure and undoubtedly the best type for a trader wishing to make a career of trading. The problem is that this fact is widely recognised and getting a space on this type of site can be a lengthy operation with average waiting lists of two to three years and in some cases as long as ten years. The market is usually an open one and stalls are supplied by the authority/operator.

Non-charter private market

Non-charter private markets are set up by private operating companies in areas where no market charter exists. Usually they are well run and fairly secure as they have been the subject of a successful planning application. Rents tend to be a touch higher than the local authority market but are usually manageable. A note of caution, though. Beware of the new markets unless they are being run by established operators. Occasionally, a landowner will realise how much rental income can be obtained from his land by allowing it to be used as a market. He therefore advertises and sets up without any form of planning application. The market opens and closes so rapidly that it passes almost unnoticed by anyone other than the trader who has lost a lot of money and the chance of better markets by supporting this one. Rarely does a market that hasn't been the subject of planning application succeed.

There is a little-known piece of legislation, the General Development Order 1963, which, under certain circumstances, allows land to be used as a market for up to 14 consecutive weeks in a year, one day per week, but that cannot be extended legally without a full planning application. I have known markets opened under this legislation which have run for up to two years, and they are useful as a stop gap where you can't find anything else for that particular day of the week.

Market halls

I have deliberately not mentioned market halls earlier for a number of reasons. Although to all intents and purposes they are markets, and are managed by a local authority or operating company, the actual administration is more akin to running a small shop, and for this reason it is unlikely that the person starting out on a market trading career would be interested in this type of operation. Apart from the fact that you leave your stock neatly displayed under lock and key in the market hall overnight, instead of loading on to your van, from the trader's point of view everything said in this book applies with one exception – the question of rent.

In a market hall it is customary for the rental to be paid on a leasehold-type basis monthly, or even three monthly, in advance. Few allow casual traders, although there are some about, and some where rent is paid on a weekly basis. These are not generally recognised markets as such, but spring up where a large department store has closed down and an enterprising businessperson has bought it and divided the space up to make a shopping arcade or market.

Sunday markets

In the early 1970s Sunday markets appeared on virtually every piece of spare land all over the country, following the repeal of the Sunday Fairs Act. Finding their own markets suffering as a result of this new phenomenon, the existing local authorities quickly retaliated by seeking injunctions in the High Court to close the markets down. The first major success was when Warwick City Council won a ruling that, for the purposes of the Shops Act, a market stall was a shop. This immediately prevented a wide range of goods from being sold legally.

From then on markets were held in various parts of the country by a large number of operators and individuals and, although most of them closed within a short time of opening because of various legal pressures, a number remained and are still operating today. The most notable are Finmere in Buckinghamshire and Bessemer Road in Cardiff. They attract literally hundreds of stalls all year round.

As a result of ongoing legislation and difficulties with these markets, the numbers have dropped drastically leaving a few good Sunday markets where trading conditions are first class, and any trader starting up is advised to take a space on the nearest one early in his career. They are all listed in *World's Fair*, as are the new markets which open almost weekly.

As far as trading is concerned, comments made previously on long-term stability in weekly markets do not apply to the Sunday market scene and you will benefit from any Sunday market, even if it is only on a one-week basis, because they are almost always heavily advertised and good crowd pullers. (See also page 22.)

Car boot sales

Car boot sales are a recent import from across the Atlantic and unlikely to be suited to the full-time career market trader. They can, however, provide useful training in the early days before you decide to commit yourself to the purchase of stock or a stall.

A car boot sale is an event where people turn up in their cars or vans and sell second-hand goods. Car boot sales were originally known as 'garage sales' and are a common sight in the United States, where every so often people clear out all their old junk and surplus household goods and have a sale in their neighbourhood.

Because these sales do not contravene the Shops Act

Sunday trading restrictions they have spread rapidly, and a glance at your local paper will always reveal several sales in your area every weekend.

As far as stock is concerned you may already have a considerable amount of old household goods lying around which you won't be using again, or you can do what a lot of 'professional' car booters are now doing and go round all the local jumble sales buying up items for sale on their stalls – or, more precisely, from their car boots. It is easy to get enough stock together from your attic and from your family, friends and neighbours to set up shop and perhaps make yourself £100 or so on a good Sunday.

Bear in mind, though, that car boot sales are not markets, and the law prohibits the sale of any new goods by way of trade. So even if you do well for a couple of weeks, don't get carried away and allow yourself to think that you have the makings of a long-term future. It is very much a 'pin-money' operation.

To the aspiring market trader, however, it can be useful training because it will take you through the motions of turning up at a site, setting your stock out for sale and, much more important, dealing on a face-to-face basis with your customers. All this will give you the confidence which is so important if you are going to be successful in your market trading.

Rent on car boot sales is considerably less than in a proper market but rightly so as the organisation and advertising costs are different, and much lower than those incurred by the market operator proper.

Becoming a trader on a car boot sale is simplicity itself. Once you have your stock, and a small table (a decorator's table from your local DIY warehouse is ideal), you simply search the columns of your local papers for the locations of current events and turn up. There is usually no pre-booking and only rarely is a contact telephone number given in the advertisement.

It is advisable to arrive at least an hour before the advertised starting time. On arrival you will be directed to where you will be standing. Your rent will either be collected as you enter the site or later by the organisers.

When setting out your goods for sale you should follow a different procedure from that for a market stall. You should set your goods out on your table as informally as possible. You are selling second-hand goods and the 'junk shop' appearance is more attractive in these circumstances.

Car boot trading can be profitable and enjoyable and a potentially lucrative short-term business. It is unlikely, however, that it will provide the stability and security which can come from a proper market stall.

Operating

If you have £500 or more available and you are a reasonable organiser you might like to consider car boot sale operating as a business. It is lucrative and relatively straightforward.

As car boot sales are a recent development there is very little legislation. They are not markets and therefore the market legislation and restrictions do not apply. However, it is vital that you preserve your sale status and by allowing any trader to sell new goods you will immediately lose that, turning your event into a market which can be closed by any local authority applying the relevant legal procedures. Having said that, a good steady income can be derived from operating these sales. All that is required is a piece of suitable land. Any piece of flat land ranging from a large public house car park to a large field is suitable. Obviously, there must be vehicular access, and your site should not be in such a position as to create a traffic hazard. Many car boot sales have been discontinued because of the traffic congestion caused.

A rent has to be negotiated with the site owner and this can be done in one of two ways. You can either negotiate a flat rent, and you should always offer to pay this weekly in advance, or you can reach an agreement whereby you pay a percentage or fee per car. The latter is a better arrangement if you are just starting up. If you charge £4 per car you may, for example, offer the site owner £1 for every car that trades.

The second agreement involves a certain amount of trust but, although it means that you will pay more out in rent if you have a well-attended sale, it has the advantage of ensuring that you will not make a loss on bad days.

Once you have your site you can advertise. There is no need to advertise separately for car booters and customers. One advertisement stating the date, time and venue will attract all the attention you need. Your advertising should be restricted to local newspapers within a 20-mile radius. Any other advertising will be wasted and represent an unnecessary drain on your finances. Never advertise your event more than one week in advance as this will simply confuse regular car booters and put off customers.

It is largely a matter of choice whether you hold your sale weekly or monthly but hold it regularly. If you decide that monthly is best, hand out leaflets to the traders at your market stating the date of the next sale clearly. If the area in which you hold your sale is well populated and can sustain a weekly event, hold a weekly sale. You will rapidly build up a regular clientele of both traders and customers.

It is vital that you advertise each and every event. There are so many sales advertised nowadays that, if you fail to advertise one week, all your potential customers will go elsewhere. That may sound an exaggerated claim but it is very much the case with this type of event.

Once the day of your sale arrives you should be at your site from early morning to marshal the first arrivals to their trading places. You will need a couple of helpers at least to direct traffic for you and generally assist you with supervising the event.

If your event is a regular one and held in a field or similar site without any of the usual basic facilities, you should consider renting a mobile toilet block. Most plant hire companies will come to a reasonable arrangement with you if they can see future regular business in the pipeline.

Likewise, if there are no refreshment facilities nearby you should allow at least one catering snack bar to attend. Only if you have a regular attendance of more than 250 booters should you have more than one refreshment unit. You can allow a caterer on your site without affecting the status of your sale and you should charge the caterer rent. This varies from area to area but you could telephone a local market operator and ask for a guideline. You should charge the same.

Once a sale is established as a regular event there is no reason why you should not also generate extra rental income from allowing someone to attend with a bouncy castle or a children's roundabout or similar attraction. Again, these will not affect the status of your event as a 'non-market' and they will provide you with extra rental income and make your event more attractive.

At the end of the day you must ensure that your site is left clean and clear of all litter. This will not only help your relations with the site owner, but will also ensure that local residents have no cause for complaint.

As with any other market-type project, you must remember that you are running a business and that the rules of good financial control and records apply as much to you as to any market operator or trader.

A good car boot sale, once up and running, should provide you with an income at the end of the day of approximately half the rentals collected, and if you consider that some sales have several hundred cars at £5 or more per car you will realise the potential on offer.

Flea markets

The flea market is a variation on the car boot sale, the difference being that it is run from proper market stalls, and market rules apply. As far as stock is concerned, no new stock is permitted, and some operators go even further by limiting stock to that which originated in a certain period. It is possible to make a good living from flea markets and if second-hand goods interest you this is the course you should take.

Most towns now have flea markets operated by the local authority or agents acting on their behalf. They are regular events offering you, as a trader, the same level of security as at a general trading market and far greater than at a car boot sale.

Unlike car boot sales, flea markets operate on normal weekdays. If you decide to follow this route, you will probably find yourself working car boot sales on Sundays as well as your mid-week flea market activities.

Shows

Another option is that provided by shows. The types of show range from your local village gala where you could have a stall for a small rent, to the giant East of England Show, the Royal Show at Stoneleigh or the Great Yorkshire Show at Harrogate, where you could pay hundreds of pounds in rent for the privilege of displaying and selling your goods.

In between the gala and the major show there is a whole range of events - steam rallies, carnivals, motor shows, agricultural shows. There are literally dozens each week.

Some traders make a seasonal career of doing just the shows, which has the advantage of an increased social life and travel. There are a lot of negatives, however, and unless you are committed to this type of operation you should be wary.

One of the main drawbacks is that shows are usually promoted only once a year, so you have to find a different show with different operators and different negotiations for every day you want to work. You will also be expected to pay your rent months in advance, so you will have a large capital sum tied up well before the beginning of the season. There are few shows which open mid-week and, by and large, these are the major agricultural and county shows which are well established. If you are lucky enough to be able to get a space you will be expected to pay a small fortune in rent. Realistically, you can expect to have your show availability limited to weekends.

If you want to work the shows you could work both markets and shows – shows at weekends in the season and markets at all the other times. Many traders operate successfully in this way and there is nothing to discourage you from doing this, though you will have to work seven days a week during the summer show season if you want to be successful.

Seasonal and holiday markets

Most coastal and holiday resorts have markets which open throughout the holiday season and they are usually good money spinners. But remember that they are seasonal and you will have to find alternative work during the closed season. You will have to weigh up whether being away from your regular markets during the holiday season will have such an adverse effect on your regular trade as to be economically unviable. The new trader will have to play it by ear for a couple of years.

Street trading

At one time street trading was widespread, but it has declined rapidly and there are now few genuine street traders. It is not an area which should be considered by anyone setting up as a market trader although, as anyone who has watched street traders will know, it is usually lucrative.

To become a street trader a licence, issued by the local authority, is required. But be warned. All local authorities have their own policies, and the vast majority do not allow any street trading whatsoever, with the remaining few issuing licences on a restricted basis.

Those authorities which do issue licences are usually in the larger cities, especially those with a tourist industry. They will issue licences to those traders whom they feel will enhance the area's atmosphere.

Before you make any investment whatsoever you should enquire if your local authority permits street trading and, if so, whether a licence will be available.

There are limited opportunities for this style of trading within privately operated shopping malls or centres, but the operators of such centres usually require a high rent. Your first enquiry should be to the manager of the individual centre who will either be in a position to make a decision himself or will need to refer to the head office.

Occasionally, you will have seen in your town centre someone setting out ties, 'jewellery', cigarette lighters, bundles of Christmas paper etc on orange boxes or milk crates. People doing this are *not* traders. They are engaging in an illegal trade. If you are thinking of becoming a trader you should avoid this type of 'operation' at all costs. Such traders are not licensed anywhere in the country. The trade name for them is 'fly-traders' and if you have watched them you will know why.

They are frequently prosecuted because they are breaking both criminal and trading laws. Because of the time it takes to go through the courts to get a conviction for breach of the trading laws, the usual method of dealing with them is for the police to arrest the 'traders' for obstruction and take them before a court the same or the next day, thus taking them off the streets and landing them with a heavy fine.

The goods sold are mostly shoddy or second class, the trader having the advantage of not being there the next day when dissatisfied customers try to redress the balance.

There is one form of street trading which, although strictly speaking illegal, is tolerated and that is the display of paintings etc by artists. Perhaps the best known example of this is alongside Green Park in Piccadilly, London.

There are also others in Hampstead and Kensington Gardens on Bayswater Road, London. These trading outlets are based on historical precedent and new traders will be unlikely to get space as it is, in fact, for artists rather than traders.

Pavement artists and buskers also fit into this category and are tolerated on a 'blind eye' basis rather than licensed to collect. While they can do fairly well in some areas, they are engaging in pin-money work and not serious careers.

Anyone who is thinking of setting up in business as a market trader is advised to steer well clear of any form of street trading because there is no long-term advantage to be gained, and it is doubtful whether there is anything to be gained in the short term – other than hassle and loss.

Chapter 5

Markets and Mobile Catering

Markets and mobile catering are closely related and so they are dealt with here under one heading; what applies to one almost invariably applies to another.

The majority of people who consider market trading as a career seem to feel that catering is the most appropriate trade to pursue. Perhaps, on the surface, this is fairly obvious; after all, everyone needs to eat, and when all the other stalls on a market are desperately scratching round for business, the caterer in his hot dog van always has a queue. And basic catering is not complicated. It doesn't take much practice to make a reasonable cup of tea or coffee, and hot dogs, hamburgers etc are even more straightforward.

Another attraction is the high profit margins. No one could fail to notice the level of profit on a cup of tea selling at, say, 30 pence.

So if catering is attractive, why doesn't everyone try it? Well, that's just the problem – most do. The result is that, every time a new market is advertised, the operator is deluged with applications for space for catering. I remember setting up a market in East Anglia some years ago. I advertised in all the local newspapers in the area and received more than 200 applications from traders for space. Of those applications, more than 130 were from caterers or would-be caterers.

Does this mean that catering is a no-go area as far as the new trader is concerned? The answer to that question depends on the individual. Perhaps the question can best be addressed by looking at how you could make a successful entry into mobile catering.

It is unlikely that you will be able to find sufficient space on the markets to make a living at the outset. You will have to persevere, get in fast when a new market opens, and trust to a large extent to luck. One good market, whether it is a Sunday or a mid-week one, will provide sufficient income to give you a reasonable weekly wage, so at least that should provide your bread. To earn the butter and jam you need other outlets and this is where mobile and market catering cross paths.

An ever-increasing number of caterers are realising the advantages of working industrial estates and this is an area where a new trader can compete on an equal footing with an established one. There are a number of new industrial estates opening up all the time in every part of the country housing small industrial units. Some have their own canteens but many are too small to have such a facility. As a caterer you can take advantage of this by finding a site for your van or trailer and setting up shop on a regular basis. You will quickly find that you are not only getting trade from people working on the site but also attracting delivery lorry drivers and salespeople and others visiting the site on a casual basis.

It is easy to find a site. You can either do so informally by finding a small corner of undeveloped land and parking there or (more acceptable and certainly more secure) canvass the firms on the site and get permission to stand on a small corner of their car park or yard. Remember that you are offering a service to the whole estate. Your site should therefore be at the roadside but not in a position to cause any obstruction to passing traffic or create any dangers from blind corners etc.

You may be asked to make a token payment if you are using someone else's land but usually you will be allowed to stand free of any rental charge.

You will probably find that your trade for the first couple of days is slow but, once people realise that you are there, that you are reliable, that your prices and the quality of your food are acceptable, you will quickly build up a regular clientele and have a secure business. You can help the business to build up more quickly by circulating notices to all the units on the estate telling potential customers of your existence. You could even build up such a good customer base that, by the time you are offered a space on a market, you might be reluctant to leave your industrial site. That is a financial decision which only you can make, based on your particular business.

Another alternative source of trade for the mobile catering unit is the roadside snack bar. Usually sited in lay-bys, these units (which until a few years ago were pursued relentlessly by some local authorities) are now positively encouraged by the Department of Transport.

When looking for sites you should look for roads which are busy with passing traffic (especially commercial vehicles), do not have a proper transport café facility nearby, and where you can site your trailer/van and not cause any traffic congestion. Remember that it isn't only your vehicle which will be parked; the drivers who are spending their money will also require parking space and their vehicles could be huge articulated tractors and trailers. Many of the better sites are now fully occupied but there are still plenty about if you care to look.

It is sensible to contact the local authority once you find a site which you feel could be suitable. They can't give you permission to stand there (no roadside operator, unless he is on private land, has actually got permission to stand) but the authority can advise you on the acceptability of the site as far as they are concerned from both a traffic, planning and hygiene point of view. You will have to register your sales unit with the authority anyway before you offer food for sale in their area – that is the law (see Chapter 8).

It can be seen that, far from being a non-starter, catering has potential and offers a number of options. As with any aspect of market trading, though, the secret ingredient is hard work.

The caterer has opportunities that other traders do not have, not the least being the fact that traders eat too. Provided a market is not overrun with catering outlets (and this is something you need to check with the operators in the private sector when you make your telephone enquiry/booking), you have a captive market already there. For that reason, when I operated catering units in the past, I always made the point of being on site and open when the ordinary traders started to arrive. They look forward to a hot snack and drink while setting up their stalls and you can sometimes make as much money in those first couple of hours as in the rest of the day. Likewise, even if members of the public are not spending on the ordinary stalls, you can be sure that they will spend on food and drink.

As the profit margins on catering are high, you may be asked to pay more rent per foot than a normal trader but it is usually well worth doing so. If I were setting up as a market trader in today's market, I would probably choose catering.

Catering vans and trailers

If you are selling food or going into catering, you will have to buy a trailer-type unit and this is where you start talking big money.

Trailers of various kinds are advertised regularly in the trade press and there is a particularly good section in *Exchange & Mart* each week. Second-hand trailers are available from as little as a few hundred pounds with new ones starting from about £1500. While choice is much determined by need, the entrepreneur can spend up to £10,000 or so on a luxury unit. Remember, though, if you have this kind of money to invest that's fine, but you need to sell a lot of cups of tea to recoup the outlay. Trailers are a legal requirement for all processed and uncooked food sales and there is no short cut.

In truth, any type of unit is suitable for the business, provided that it is clean and equipped in accordance with the appropriate food and hygiene regulations (see pages 69–76). But the more you can afford to spend on a unit the better. Appearance counts and people are far more likely to spend at an attractive, clean-looking food outlet than at a converted caravan, no matter how clean it might be. That isn't to say that if you can only afford a second-hand conversion you will fail. To achieve the maximum potential from catering you should aim to acquire a good-looking purpose-built unit as quickly as possible. You will certainly notice the increase in your turnover.

As far as operating the unit is concerned, you should go through the same preliminaries as you would in any other trade. Check that you have everything you need before you set out from your base, and don't forget a good supply of fresh water unless you already know that there is a supply on site.

Don't over-order. You are dealing with perishable foodstuffs. It is better to run out early for a few weeks until you find your level than have to throw away a large amount of potential profit on wasted stock.

When deciding what to sell, keep it simple. You could probably sell full steak meals at lunch-time to the traders but the amount of effort required to prepare them makes the idea unrealistic. You shouldn't be afraid to experiment, though, and try to come up with items that others can't offer.

A catering unit of any kind, because it has water boilers and cooking pans and limited space, soon becomes very hot and you shouldn't stock anything, such as chocolate, which is affected by heat. You should ensure that if you are planning to sell cold drinks you have a built-in refrigerator, otherwise limit stocks of drinks to the lowest level possible.

Make sure that you have adequate waste paper sacks or bins for the outside of your unit. The waste generated will be far greater than for any other type of stall and all operators, whether in the public or private sector, will expect you to accept responsibility for the area surrounding your unit.

At present-day levels you can expect to be able to stock your unit comfortably for the first day's trading for as little as £200 or even less, depending on the volume of trade expected.

Barbecues are on the increase at markets at the moment. They are not operated from a catering unit but from an ordinary walk-through stall which has a barbecue inside it. If you go in for this type of barbecue you should be cautious. You are required to maintain exactly the same standards as any other food outlet, which includes offering your stall for inspection. Failure to do so can be expensive and the risks of handling meats, cooked and uncooked, are many. Unless you are fully experienced in barbecues and food handling, you should not even consider this type of operation.

Of the many barbecue suppliers, the foremost is Westlers, an American company with a strong British sales operation which sells not only the type of goods the caterer will need but also offers worthwhile informal advice to its customers.

Wherever possible, avoid using frozen meat products. Use canned foods instead; they not only keep better but, if unsold and unopened, they can be kept for several weeks in normal conditions.

Chapter 6
Market Operating

In many ways, market operating is far more complex than trading, but at the same time it is easier, and can certainly be much more profitable. You only have to look at one of the larger Sunday markets with, say, 400 stalls at £15 per day minimum rent to get an idea of the kind of money we are talking about.

The first requisite to market operating is finding a site. Those already in operation range from car parks and farm fields to disused airfields and county showgrounds. The range is endless; any flat piece of land more than three or four acres in area can be used for a market.

Having identified the site and negotiated a rent with the owner you can go one of two ways. Which path you choose will depend on your financial status.

The *proper method* is to approach the local authority where the land is situated and apply for planning permission. Subject to certain conditions, you could in fact open up your market for up to 14 weeks under planning legislation (the General Development Order 1963), pending the full planning application. It has to be said that local authorities, especially those which operate markets themselves, rarely grant planning permission for a market so, if you are following this course, you will have to be patient and try for a number of sites before you are lucky.

Before you even apply for planning permission you must do some basic research. First, you will have to ascertain if your proposed market contravenes any charter rights owned by the local authority. These are the ancient charters, granted through the ages for various lords of the manor and subsequently sold to the local authorities, allowing the charter holder to be the only person or organisation operating a market in a stated area.

The High Court has ruled that where such a charter exists no outsider can operate a market within 6⅔ miles of the charter market. Even this is open to several interpretations and some High Court rulings have made the 6⅔ miles extend from the market operating authorities' boundaries rather than from the market itself. Whichever rules apply, penalties for breach of charter rights can be heavy, resulting in the operator not only being ordered to hand over all his income from the 'pirate' market but also to pay court costs and exemplary damages.

Charter holders will invariably be granted injunctions preventing the named person from operating any market in their area; if he should do so the authority is entitled to apply for him to be committed to prison for contempt of court – swingeing penalties for anyone just starting out on their own.

However, charter rights may not be held over the site you are looking at and if that is the case your next task is to find out whether the local authority has the power to require the notification and registration of markets in its area. Certain authorities which have adopted the measures of the Local Government Act can so demand and, if you go ahead and open without notifying them, you can again be subject to considerable financial penalties from the courts.

If you are totally clear on both these points you can make your planning application. The planning authority has to consider your application purely on planning grounds, and therefore the fact that you are applying for permission to open a Sunday market, which would in itself be in contravention of certain parts of the 1950 Shops Act and so illegal, must not be considered by the planners in reaching their decision. Your planning application must be considered on planning grounds alone and that means such things as traffic problems, the suitability of the site, and the effect your proposal would have on the neighbourhood and environment.

An operator who has applied for permission for a mid-week market which fits in with a town centre development, or who has permission from the charter holder, will be much more likely to succeed, and operators with planning permission have a good secure business waiting for them.

The *alternative method* is the most usual one. The establishment would call these markets pirate markets and the operators pirate operators, but that doesn't mean they are all rogues. Indeed, many operations which could be called 'pirate', where operators open up market sites with no regard to any of the planning laws, are, in fact, big business.

However, you must be wary about opening in breach of charter rights and local government legislation; it can be expensive and it is not worthwhile. What you need to do is research the local authorities carefully and find out which have a liberal view of markets and try to find sites in their areas. They do exist and a market in such an area will usually attract little local authority attention.

Enforcement of the Shops Act is confused at the moment but most authorities, in view of recent High Court and European Court decisions, are adopting a wait-and-see stance which is useful for the market operator. In fact, by operating a market where goods prohibited by the Shops Act are sold, the operator is not committing an offence unless it can be proved, and all efforts in the past 20 years have failed to prove, that he has knowledge that a particular transaction is in breach of the Act. Theoretically, it could be argued that he aided and abetted the trader to make the sale and is therefore guilty of an offence. This is a case of taking a sledgehammer to crack a nut, and thus far such a prosecution has failed on the rare occasions when it has been attempted. (More on this in Chapter 8, page 65.)

Sunday trading

Let us assume that you have found a site with no legal problems in an area where the local authority turns a blind eye on Sunday trading. What do you do next?

You are faced with two tasks. First, to get traders for your market and, second, to get members of the public, the punters, to attend.

Clearly, both these tasks involve advertising. The first job, getting the traders, is easy. There are so many traders looking for spaces that you won't have any problems at all (see Chapter 9).

To advertise for the public, one decent-sized advertisement in the local press on the Friday and Saturday before the market opens will have a good response. On an ongoing basis, local radio produces results and for big markets you should try television. You must work to a budget, though. It is pointless spending £10,000 on advertising an event which is only going to produce half that in revenue.

As well as paid advertising keep an eye out for free publicity in the local media. Send them a release about the market opening – you might get a mention. Offer a local charity the chance of a free stall and then persuade the local newspaper to come along and take a photograph.

Once you are well established, your local radio station might be interested in attending the market with its own roadshow to do an outside broadcast. When I was operating a few years ago I had a bonus. The local bus company, without any reference to me, printed small posters which were placed on every bus in the fleet, advertising bus services to the market. This was some of the best advertising I'd ever had. Not only did I know nothing about it, it hadn't cost me anything either!

Come the day of the market you will have your hands full. You will have to allocate spaces to all the traders who turn up, and they will all want to be on the same corner. You must be forceful, allocate spaces, and ensure that traders go to their allotted spaces.

You will need at least a couple of staff working for you and, as your rental income is going to be a large sum, they must be people you can trust.

As far as rent collecting is concerned you should collect a fixed amount at the gate, that amount being the minimum you have specified for rent, usually in the region of £10–£15 (1992 rates). The advantage of collecting at the gate is that it is quicker and safer and no one can get through the gate without paying. Once your market is up and running you can send one of your colleagues round to collect any balance of rent owed where traders have more than the minimum space.

If the market is organised properly, traders should get away quickly at the end of the day, and then all you have to do is ensure that the site is left clean. A couple of casual labourers will usually tidy up the site for a reasonable payment.

Any signs that you put at the roadside, or on your site, advertising your market, should, strictly speaking, have planning permission and if the council tries to obstruct your operation (and many councils do) it could cause you a great deal of inconvenience. There is no legal way for you to put up signs, even temporary ones. It is therefore in your interests, if you put up signs, to do so as tidily and inoffensively as possible.

If you engage in 'fly-posting', the practice of sticking posters on any available space, you could be liable for heavy financial penalties, based on a fine for each poster displayed and an ongoing penalty for each day the poster remains. You should, if possible, confine your displays to the windows of buildings, houses, shops, factories etc, where you are within your rights.

As a rule of thumb, apart from traffic-directing signs (which most authorities will not object to, provided the signs themselves don't create a traffic hazard) you don't need posters. The best form of advertising is via your local newspaper, radio or television station.

Market operating can be a headache but when successful it can be very profitable, realising sometimes thousands of pounds in a day.

Scotland

The law in Scotland is somewhat different as far as private operators are concerned and, while there are no Sunday trading restrictions, all market operators are required to register with the local authority in whose area they wish to operate and it is a criminal offence not to do so. The registration form is complex and requests, apart from all the usual information, details of any criminal record and other markets operated. A person who is not a substantial businessperson and cannot give evidence of a track record in market operating will not normally be registered.

There is currently no Shops Act in Scotland which restricts Sunday trading.

Conclusion

One of the most successful operating companies, and one of the first, is Spook Erection, a company based in the Cotswolds. In the early days of 'pirate' markets they operated a number of markets in various parts of England. They have now developed considerably and only operate fully legal markets with planning permission. They operate a number of mid-week markets in England and they also have a substantial Scottish operation, and the jewel in their crown is undoubtedly the Sunday market at the showground at Ingleston near Edinburgh, a market which holds the record for the number of traders on one site on one day at well over 2000 traders.

Arguably the largest Sunday market in England is the one at Finmere in Buckinghamshire, operated since the early 1970s by Wendy Fair of Ruislip, Middlesex. Several companies operate 400–500 stall markets such as the market at Castle Donington in the East Midlands, operated by Gramlo, and there are several others in different parts of the country. Anyone considering setting up as a market operator would visit as many markets as possible to study how other people run their events. There is a strong element of competition between operators and I suggest that such visits are made incognito.

There is now an organisation of private market operators: the Association of Private Market Operators (APMO) (see Appendix 1 for details).

Chapter 7

Suppliers

Suppliers are almost as numerous and varied as traders themselves, ranging from small one-man operated shop-front type wholesalers to multi-branch operations. When you first start up, visit as many as possible before committing yourself.

As a market trader you will be looked upon, quite erroneously, as a less secure and reliable businessperson than the small shopkeeper or businessperson with premises. I mention this because it is unlikely that any request for credit facilities, certainly in the early stages, will be granted. Although this may seem inconvenient, it can in fact be helpful because it means that you can't build millstones round your neck for over-stocking. There is nothing like counting out and parting with your own cash to teach you restraint.

Unless you are dealing in a trade where you already have first-class knowledge of suppliers and manufacturers, as a new market trader you would be well advised to deal with a wholesaler who specialises in supplying the markets. There are many such wholesalers in all areas of the country, although they are particularly plentiful in the larger conurbations.

There are some areas where various trades are gathered together. For example, in Manchester there are a large number of clothing warehouses and jewellery wholesalers. Generally speaking, gifts, fancy goods and watches etc are congregated in the East End of London. Nottingham seems to attract warehouses with household goods and textiles. The West Midlands have some excellent large general wholesale warehouses.

This doesn't mean that you can only find those goods in those areas. Every town and city has its warehouses and you will find all you want, unless you are specialising in a very narrow field, in your own backyard.

Many warehouses have a minimum amount that you must spend at any one time, and most will require proof of

the fact that you are, or are setting up as, a bona fide
market trader.

When you buy your stock from a warehouse you must
remember that your fellow traders are also likely to shop
there; don't automatically think that the advertised bargains are as attractive as they seem. If there was some way
you could guarantee that you were the only trader with a
particular item, it would be fine. But unless that is the case,
be wary.

You could advertise in the classified columns of your
regional newspaper for surplus stocks, in the hope that
other businesses which have over-stocked, or manufacturers who have come to the end of a production line, will offer
you their remainders. It is useful if you have funds to get
into this side of the business because you can pick up goods
at ridiculously low prices. You are then in a position to pass
savings on to your customers.

Remember that each time you make a stock purchase
you must have the proper documentation, ie a receipt and
an invoice showing the payment made and the goods paid
for. Most goods have VAT charged on them and you will be
expected to charge VAT when you sell them which you will
be expected to account for (if you turn over £36,600 or
more per year). If you failed to get a VAT receipt at the time
of purchase you can end up badly out of pocket. (We dealt
with these matters in detail in Chapter 3.)

It is also important for legal reasons that you can
account for the purchase of all your stock if called on to do
so. Crime is on the increase and although it may not affect
you directly it could do so indirectly. Suppose a large
amount of your stock is similar to that stolen in a burglary.
The victim of the burglary walks round the market and sees
your stock looking suspiciously like what he's lost. A quick
phone call and you could find yourself having to explain to
the local constabulary where you obtained the goods. If all
your documentation is in order you will have no problem,
but if you've failed to take the necessary precautions you
can imagine what would happen next – all because you
forgot to ask for an invoice. Your accountant will also be
unable to work satisfactorily if he hasn't the full documentation for all your business operations.

When you are conducting your market research as far as
stock purchasing is concerned, you could do worse than
find out if the owner or director of the wholesaler comes

from a markets background. A great many do, and are particularly helpful when giving advice to new traders. Don't be afraid to ask - their business depends on people like you running a successful operation and they are always happy to help.

Warehouses advertise regularly in the trade press and are listed in *The Markets Year Book*.

Your buying should be an organised part of your business. Don't just go to the warehouse when your stock levels demand a trip. Make at least one day each week your buying day and use it for that purpose alone. Don't stick to one warehouse. Keep your eyes open for others in the area and select the bargains from each. That way you are taking advantage of the buying power and business of a number of warehouses and can pass bargains on to your customers.

Chapter 8

The Law

The market trader has the same legal responsibilities as any other businessperson, plus several additional requirements by virtue of the fact that he is trading out of doors.

Shops Act 1950

In the case of *Warwick City Council v Maby* in the early 1970s, the High Court ruled that within the terms of the Shops Act, a stall is a shop. The same ruling also includes vans, where the van sells from a fixed point on a market as opposed to the mobile shop which moves from place to place during its selling day.

This ruling came about when counsel for Mr Maby and his company, Spook Erection, submitted that the terms of the Shops Act, with regard to Sunday trading restrictions, did not apply to stalls which were not permanent structures, and therefore not shops within the terms of the Act – a submission which was overruled.

The Shops Act 1950, which incidentally is under constant debate and is likely to be changed in the not too distant future, states that it is illegal to trade on Sundays for retail purposes except in certain cases. These exceptions are listed in Schedule 5 of the Act. The list includes periodicals, some perishable foodstuffs, car accessories, gifts and souvenirs. Surprisingly, you are not allowed to sell copies of the Bible on Sundays because it is a book and not a periodical.

There are also exceptions in areas which have holiday resort status where, for 18 consecutive Sundays during the holiday season, goods can be sold openly.

Enforcement of the Shops Act is in the hands of the district councils and each has its own policy as far as this duty is concerned. Such is the confusion surrounding Sunday trading, with rulings made at an ever-increasing rate in the European Court, that a large number of authorities are effectively turning a blind eye to any breaches of the Act within their area. These are the areas where Sunday markets are most likely to trade untroubled by legal problems.

But any council receiving a complaint from a resident about breaches of the Act does have a legal responsibility to act on that complaint, and could be subject to legal sanctions if it failed to do so.

As far as the individual trader is concerned, it is a matter of choice. In an area where a Sunday market operates you should be fairly safe from action. In the early days of Sunday markets, in the early 1970s when the Sunday Fairs Act was first repealed, local authorities used to act against markets by visiting the market 'en masse' and prosecuting individual traders through the magistrates courts for breaches of the regulations. There was rarely a defence, and conviction led to fines of around £100, although this varied from one area to another.

These same authorities quickly realised, however, that going through the courts was a lengthy process and in many cases fines were ineffective compared to the profits which could be made on a good market.

Armed with the details of the convictions, the authority had to apply to the High Court for an injunction to close the market and prevent the operator from opening another market within the authority's area.

It didn't take long for a bright lawyer in one of the local authorities to realise that the same could be achieved much more quickly without going through the magistrates court. The new procedure was for members of the Trading Standards or Environmental Health Departments to visit the market, note that breaches of the Act were taking place and swear out affidavits to the effect that they had seen breaches of the law. The High Court would then on request grant an injunction in the same way as before, closing the market and preventing the operator from opening anywhere in that council's area in the future, or at least while the injunction was in existence.

The result is that the individual trader is now safer from prosecution than before. In fact, for the past ten years or so there have been few prosecutions of individual traders for breaches of the 1950 Shops Act.

Sale of Goods Act 1979

Most of your market trade will be done for cash, and when cash changes hands in exchange for goods the terms of the 1979 Sale of Goods Act apply.

Goods offered to the consumer must be suitable for the purpose for which they are sold and must correspond with any samples, descriptions or display items.

If you are offering any goods including goods which are 'seconds' or 'slight imperfects' where the price is accordingly low, the customer cannot claim for defects if (a) the defect is pointed out at the time of sale, or (b) the customer is allowed to examine the goods before making a purchase. This applies to individual items and a general disclaimer notice on your stall has no legal standing whatsoever and, indeed, is illegal under the Unfair Contract Terms Act 1977. However large the print on a notice displayed on your stall, it does not remove any of your obligations to the customer.

If you accept a deposit from a customer on a particular item you must reserve that item and you are liable to civil action if you fail to do so. If you do trade in this way, you must always make sure that both you and your customer agree a time limit for how long the goods will be held. Failure to do so could result in much legal argument.

When you sell a specific item to a customer, ownership passes from you to your customer at the following points in a transaction:

(a) A finished specific article in a deliverable state is the buyer's as soon as his offer is accepted, whatever the time of payment or delivery.

(b) If the trader has to put the goods into a deliverable state by, for example, weighing them to ascertain the price, they become the buyer's property when he is notified that they are ready for delivery.

Consumer Protection Act 1987

Under the terms of the Consumer Protection Act 1987 it is an offence to infringe safety regulations that apply to some manufactured goods. However, when such infringements take place it is the manufacturer who is responsible in law, and not the retailer.

Misrepresentation

If you deliberately mislead your customer in order to close a deal, you may be liable to a claim for damages as well as having to reimburse the customer for the cost of the goods. The customer will have to prove that you deliberately misrepresented. The law recognises that we are none of us perfect and if you are careless or genuinely mistaken, your liability will be restricted to reimbursement of the cost of the goods.

The Trade Descriptions Act 1968 applies to any form of description, be it an oral or written statement or an advertisement. The statement must be false and this includes situations where the customer is misled into buying the goods.

The rules apply to unfair pricing and particularly to misleading indications of British or European Community origin on imported goods.

The County Council's Trading Standards Department is the body responsible for enforcement of the Act and it is authorised to make test purchases or to seize goods from your stall to ascertain whether an offence has been committed.

Normally the Department only acts where they have received a specific complaint from a member of the public but increasingly the department's officers are 'raiding' market stalls where they suspect 'pirate' copies of video and/or audio tapes are being offered for sale.

Misleading bargain offers

Misleading bargain offers are prohibited under the Consumer Protection Act 1987. Traders must not offer mythical bargains which use false comparisons. Genuine comparisons are, of course, still legal and these may include comparisons with past or future prices, prices charged by other named traders or stores, and comparisons with recommended retail prices, except where this is specifically prohibited under other legislation.

All aspects of markets, rival markets, and rules and regulations relating to the running and control of privately owned markets are covered fully in Pease and Chitty's *Law of Markets and Fairs* (Tolley Publishing).

The market caterer

The law for the caterer is much more complex and detailed knowledge is necessary before you start trading. Your local Environmental Health Officer will advise you on any requirements and up-to-date legislation as far as the sale and supply of food and drink are concerned.

Basically, the law covers three separate categories: the product, the premises and the people.

As far as the product is concerned the terms of the Trade Descriptions Act apply and false and misleading statements should not be made.

The Price Marking (Food and Drink on Premises) Order 1979 applies to the mobile catering unit and provides that the price of all goods on offer must be prominently displayed so customers are fully aware of the cost of food and drink *before* they order it. Similar provisions apply to stalls, mobile grocery and ice-cream vans under the Price Marking (Food) Order 1978.

The Order defines two areas:

1. The eating area where table service of any kind is provided. The display of prices muist be situated near the entrance to the premises so that customers can see and read before eating.
2. The supply area. The display must be located behind the counter or bar from which customers are served. This applies to mobile units.

The condition of the product is determined by the Food Act 1984 under which anyone producing or selling food intended for, but unfit for, human consumption is guilty of a criminal offence, and food must be of the 'nature, substance or quality' demanded by the reasonable purchaser.

The Sale of Goods Act 1979 applies to the sale of goods by description and in this respect a contract is entered into by the caterer when he accepts the order of a customer for food or drink.

There is a wide range of legislation which applies to food premises and, as far as the law is concerned, the mobile food unit is classed as food premises.

You must not carry on any catering business at dirty premises or at any place where there is a risk of contamination.

Your premises are controlled by the Food Hygiene (General) Regulations 1970, the Food Act, the Food Hygiene (Markets, Stalls and Delivery Vehicles) Regulations 1966 and Amendment Regulations 1966.

Before you can trade, your mobile unit must be inspected and passed as suitable by the local Environmental Health Officer. Your local authority may make a charge for the inspector to visit you to carry out this work.

You are committing an offence if you offer food for sale from any unit which has not been inspected and approved by the local Environmental Health Officer. This means that if you trade in Chesterfield, for example, and the Chesterfield Borough Council Environmental Health Officer approves your sales unit you can only trade in that area. If you travel a couple of miles down the road to Clay Cross you will have to make a fresh application for a new inspection to the North East Derbyshire District Council. This applies to every single authority and is important.

The same law applies when you set up a stall as a mobile barbecue using a tent and stall. Your 'premises' must be inspected and approved.

The expression stall is given a wide meaning in law. It includes any stand, marquee, tent, mobile canteen, vehicle (whether movable or not), vending machine, site or pitch, from which food is sold.

The law as far as market caterers are concerned is governed additionally by the provisions of the Food Safety Act 1990 and the regulations apply to any trade or food business for the purpose of which a delivery vehicle is used. The definition of the handling of food means the carrying out of any operation in the sale of food, or in its preparation, transport, storage, packaging, wrapping, exposure for sale, service or delivery, and includes the cleaning of articles of equipment with which the food comes into contact. This does not apply to specific 'open foods' as discussed below.

The term market is generally as understood, but if any room which is part of the market premises is used for the purposes of a food business and any person engages therein in the handling of food it becomes a 'food room' and is subject to more stringent control under the regulations. If a food business consists wholly or partly of the supply of food intended by the supplier for immediate consumption it becomes a catering business.

The regulations differ on whether the food is 'covered food' or 'open food'. 'Covered food' is anything which is not 'open food' and 'open food' is food which has not been placed in any container of such materials and so closed as to exclude risk of contamination. Some specific foods, which could be considered as 'open food', are not to be so considered when contained within their traditional or conventional wrappers. The foods specifically mentioned in this respect are butter, hessian or jute; fish, vegetables, flour, confectionery and bakery goods, ice cream and ice lollies.

When delivery vans are used for the sale of food, they become stalls and are subject to the law as it applies to stalls.

The regulations applying to all premises and vehicles are as follows:

- Stalls must have displayed on them the name and address of the person carrying on the business and also any other address at which the stall may be kept. Stalls must not be kept at any place where they are likely to become insanitary or where they cannot be properly cleaned; when not in use they must not be stored with any food unless the food can be kept clean and free from any contamination.

- The use of stalls as sleeping places is forbidden.

- Every sanitary convenience used in connection with any market or stall must be kept clean and in good working order. Rooms in which such sanitary conveniences are installed must also be kept clean and suitably or sufficiently lighted and ventilated. Under no circumstances must such rooms be used as food rooms. In a prominent position near at hand there must be a notice displayed requesting persons to wash their hands after using the convenience.

- There must be a constant and sufficient supply of clean and wholesome water in every market or stall at or from which the food business is carried on. Wash-hand basins must be provided for the use of those engaged in the handling of food on every stall, and in connection therewith there must be provided a supply of hot water at a suitably controlled temperature with soap, towel and nailbrushes.

- In addition to these wash basins there must be sufficient sinks or other facilities for washing food and equipment used in connection with the food business carried on from the stall. These must be provided with a supply of either hot and cold water or of hot water at a suitably controlled temperature. A supply of cold water is, however, sufficient for the washing of fish, fruit or vegetables. Cold water is also sufficient for the washing of drinking vessels provided a suitable bactericide is used in the water.

- Sinks and other facilities must be kept clean and in good working order and soap or detergent must be supplied together with clean cloths or other adequate and suitable cleaning and drying facilities.

- Every stall at, or from which, open food other than vegetables is sold shall, if not in a covered market, be suitably covered and screened at the sides and back so as to prevent any contaminating substance being deposited on to the food. If the stall designed, constructed and operated in such a way as to ensure that all the food is completely enclosed until it is taken from its enclosure to be sold or cooked for immediate consumption, it need not be further screened.

- Every stall from which a food business is carried on must be suitably and sufficiently lighted.

- A sufficient number of suitably covered receptacles must be provided at every stall for waste trimmings, refuse and rubbish. Such receptacles must be constructed of impervious materials and replaced as often as necessary to prevent accumulations of obnoxious matter. They must be kept apart from food intended for sale for human consumption.

- No refuse or filth of any kind must be allowed to accumulate at any stall or in any market from which a food business is carried on.

Local authorities have their own codes of practice as far as mobile catering units are concerned and, although these may differ slightly in wording, the requirements are basically the same.

A mobile catering unit can be any of a wide range of vehicles and stalls (and/or trailers or vehicles) and including caravans from which refreshments are sold. Examples are fish and chip vans, hot dog vans and snack bar vans, commonly found either on markets or in lay-bys (see Chapter 5).

If you intend to equip a vehicle to use as a mobile catering unit you are advised to contact the local authority in whose area you intend to operate. The Environmental Health Officer of that authority will advise and assist you wherever possible.

You will be required to register as a hawker of food with the authority and charges are usually made for this registration. Depending on how you use your unit you may also need to obtain a street trader's licence. Again this is issued by the local authority and your own authority will advise you on whether this applies to you.

Gas cylinders

If you are cooking food or heating water it is likely that you will be using liquified petroleum gas (LPG) and there are a number of statutory regulations with regard to its use, including the Gas (Installation and Servicing) Regulations 1984.

LPG is supplied as a liquid under pressure in steel containers of various sizes. Leakages from the container will produce a large volume of highly inflammable gas. A small amount of gas when mixed with air will produce a larger volume of explosive mixture. The gas is heavier than air and therefore collects at low levels where it will not disperse easily, particularly in an unventilated unit.

LPG usually contains an odorant which gives it a fishy smell enabling it to be detected.

Storage on catering units

In most cases, storage of gas cylinders must be outside the unit in a suitably ventilated housing made of fire resistant material and gas tight to the interior of the unit/vehicle. It must be big enough to house all cylinders carried (including spares) but they must be kept to a minimum. Adequate ventilation must be provided to the housing at both high and low levels – a minimum of 27 square inches (168 sq cms). Openings must be fly-screened.

The housing must have a sign attached to its exterior indicating the presence of LPG; it must be lockable.

Gas cylinders may be located outside the vehicle on the following conditions: that the cylinders are secure and tamper proof; that they are stored with the valve upright; that they are not stored within 1 metre of any opening to the unit or source of ignition; all flexible tubing is kept to a minimum.

All pipework and fittings must be as short and accessible as possible and, where feasible, made of a suitable metal. These include solid drawn copper, steel tube or stainless steel tube used with suitable fittings and jointing compound.

All appliances must be secured to the unit and fitted with flame-failure devices to all burners. They must be fitted with an accessible shut-off valve or tap on the pipework immediately before it reaches the appliance. They must be positioned so as not to obstruct means of escape in case of fire.

In particular, fryers must have a canopy or hood incorporating a flue to the external air fitted with grease filters and the canopy must be big enough to cover the cooking area of the applicance. All fryers must have *either* a gas shut-off valve, temperature gauge and alarm *or* a high temperature cut-out device to the main burner.

Refrigerators should, if possible, be battery operated. However, fridges fuelled by LPG must be fitted with a flame-failure device secured to the vehicle/unit and not show a naked flame. There must be an additional air intake in the floor or wall at the base of the appliance, sited to prevent draughts extinguishing the burner or pilot flame.

There must be adequate ventilation to all units. Poor or incomplete combustion can lead to a build-up of carbon monoxide gas which can cause death. The ventilation must be capable of dispersing such a build-up.

Safety instructions
Never test for leaks with a naked light.

Always turn off the gas supply when appliances are not in use or a leak is suspected.

Do *not* operate any electrical equipment if a leak is suspected.

Extinguish nearby sources of ignition if a leak is suspected.

Fire fighting precautions

A written procedure to be followed in the event of fire must be displayed in the unit and staff must be instructed accordingly.

At least one dry powder extinguisher must be provided in a convenient position.

Health and hygiene

First aid box

At every stall from which a food business is carried on a supply of bandages, dressings (including waterproof dressings) and antiseptics for first aid treatment must be provided and maintained. Wounds must be covered at all times.

The minimum requirements for your first aid box, as laid down in the Health and Safety (First Aid) Regulations 1981, are as follows:

Item	Quantity
Guidance card or leaflet	1
Individually wrapped sterile adhesive dressings (plasters)	10
Sterile eye pads, with attachment	1
Triangular bandages (if possible sterile)	1
Sterile coverings for serious wounds	1
Safety pins	6
Medium-sized sterile unmedicated dressings approx 10 cms × 8 cms	3
Large sterile unmedicated dressings approx 13 cms × 9 cms	1
Extra large sterile unmedicated dressings 28 cms × 17.5 cms	1

If tap water is not available, sterile water or sterile normal saline in disposable containers (each holding at least 300 ml) needs to be kept near the first aid box.

Hygiene

Whether you are employing staff or operating your stall yourself you are responsible for personal hygiene.

You should ensure that people serving or preparing food on your stall are wearing suitable clean and washable overclothing.

All parts of the body likely to come into contact with food must be kept clean.

Food handlers must notify their employer immediately if they are suffering from, or are a carrier of, typhoid fever, paratyphoid fever or any other salmonella infection or amoebic dysentery or staphylococcal infection likely to cause food poisoning. It is then the responsibility of the employer or of self-employed persons to notify the district community physician.

To protect food from risk of contamination you should, as far as practicable, keep it covered during preparation and while it is displayed for sale. For example, where food is displayed at the front of the stall a 'sneeze guard' or perspex screen should be provided.

All food displayed for sale outside the stall must be placed at lest 18 inches above the ground.

Raw foods and foods which have been pre-cooked must be stored separately at all times and utensils used in the preparation and serving of raw foods must be washed thoroughly before they are used on cooked foods.

Temperature control is also important in food handling and the following foods must be stored at temperatures at or below 8°C: soft cheeses, pâtés; cooked products containing such items; sandwiches or rolls containing the above. As from 1 April 1993 all the foods in the above list must be stored at below 5°C.

Chapter 9

Publicity and Advertising

As a market trader you will have little need to advertise. In fact, all the advertising you need will come from your name and address board displayed over your stall. Therefore, unlike most other businesses, you don't need to write any advertising budget into your business plan or projection.

Publicity is intended to attract attention or promote business. The market trader is in the unique position of having his business promoted by someone else – the market operator.

From time to time your local newspaper will carry advertising features to attract shoppers to the market generally. When this happens it is likely that one of their advertising sales representatives will approach you about advertising your particular stall or product. As a way of promoting your business directly this is an absolute non-starter and could be considered a total waste of money. But, and it is a very important but, as a way of promoting the market generally these features are usually successful and, because the more people who visit your market the better, they are worthwhile for your individual business. Because you are part of the market community you would be contributing to the overall trade and this is a good thing. Such features only appear once or twice a year and individual trader advertising space is small, so the sum involved is almost negligible in terms of your annual turnover – as little as £10 or £12 sometimes. Any trader who is offered this kind of promotion should certainly take part.

Some market operators, when opening a new market, require traders to make a small one-off payment towards the cost of advertising the event, and if you want a stall at the market you have no choice but to contribute. This practice is nowhere near as common as it was ten years ago and the contribution is usually a small price to pay to guarantee your place.

The operator is in a totally different position. It is his

duty and responsibility to ensure that the market is well supported by shoppers, both for the benefit of the individual traders and for ensuring the market's long-term success.

The market must be heavily promoted in its early days and must continue to be promoted from time to time in the future. When opening a new market the operator has two tasks: first, to attract traders to the market and, second, to attract shoppers.

Attracting traders is relatively easy. All that is needed is a campaign of three or four advertisements in *World's Fair* in the weeks leading up to the market's opening date (I've always found that a quarter page is ideal). By advertising in *World's Fair* you will have avoided the need for expensive advertising in your local papers, which don't have anywhere near the same response. An example of the type of advertisement which has always had good results for me, and for many other operators, appears on page 79.

The following examples show specimens of the type of copy required for advertising. The newspapers themselves will prepare artwork, perhaps showing market stalls, or whatever, to make them look visually attractive. The venues and dates and all other contents of the examples are fictional.

Once you are established as an operator it is worth creating a file with contact details of your traders. Then when you open another market you can contact your established trader base and have the nucleus of a market before your first advertisement appears.

Advertising for traders

Calling all traders!

HUGE NEW SUNDAY MARKET

Opening Sunday, 28 February

Nottingham Castle Grounds

Smith Square

Nottingham

All hard standing,

toilets and catering on site

VACANCIES ALL TRADES

PHONE MAGNIFICENT MARKETS

071-000 0000

for full details

In this example everything the trader needs to know is shown clearly and succinctly.

Advertising for shoppers

Make shopping fun, this Sunday

visit

NOTTINGHAM SUNDAY MARKET

THIS SUNDAY 31 OCTOBER AND EVERY SUNDAY

9.00 am–4.00 pm

Hundreds of stalls, thousands of bargains

Free car parking and toilets on site

Castle Grounds, Smith Square, Nottingham

Advertising your market to the general public is a completely different operation and can be expensive if you don't keep careful control of your budget. Common sense dictates that you don't spend £10,000 on advertising a market which is only going to generate half that amount in profit.

In the example above, note that the important points are all mentioned – date, time, place and social facilities, ie car parking and toilets.

Advertising in a publication which appears more than a week before the market takes place is a total waste of money and effort. Advertisements which justifiably contain the words 'this Sunday' *will* work – no others will.

Obviously, a campaign needs to vary from area to area but there are some general rules.

Classified advertising, ie small advertisements in columns of print, does not work and is a waste of money in the context of promoting markets. A series of small display advertisements does not work either.

I once opened a market in the East Midlands and, because of a mix-up at the offices of the local evening paper, my advertising schedule was lost. The result was that all the advertising I had for that market was a large single insertion on the coming events page on the Friday before the market, which took place on the Sunday. It was the largest on the page. The result was chaos: traffic jams for three miles in either direction and a brilliant business day for everyone.

Another of my markets which was consistently success-ful was advertised by one single large display advertise-ment in one free newspaper each week. Police estimates were of approximately 20,000 shoppers flocking to the market every week.

Ongoing advertising is necessary and my most successful market was promoted by a series of short, ten-second advertisements on the local commercial radio station broadcast throughout the Saturday afternoon of each week. At the time the total cost was less than £200 and the results were out of this world. Here is a sample of the script for that type of promotion: 'For a good day out, and for all your shopping needs, visit Nottingham Sunday Market, Castle Grounds, Smith Square, Nottingham this Sunday and every Sunday.' Read that through aloud and time yourself with a stop watch. It can just fit into ten seconds.

A successful operator will also look for good public relations as well as paid advertising. This will come if the market is well laid out and properly run and if the traders and the goods sold are carefully policed.

As an operator I found it beneficial to allocate a free stall space each week to a charity. First, the charity's stall often had a mention in the local paper; sometimes a photo-grapher would visit the stall to take pictures for the news section of the paper. Second, the charity always ensured that as many as possible of its own supporters visited the market and, naturally, those doing so didn't just visit the charity stall.

Television advertising can also be useful but only if your market is fairly extensive and well established. Remember that any television transmission goes out over a large region and your image will suffer if you advertise a market on television which attracts people from a good distance away and they arrive at the site to find only a dozen or so traders.

Television advertising is expensive, but it is possible to buy enough air space for a couple of seven-second shots mid-evening the day before your market – you will certainly attract the crowds. The mechanics of producing such an advertisement are simple and will be taken care of by the television company. It will prepare an artwork or transparency slide with details of the market on a market-type background. An announcer will then read the 'voice over' text giving the same details that appear on screen. Seven seconds doesn't sound long but the air space works well.

As an approximation, you should reckon on spending a third of your potential rental income on your advertising budget in the early stages; this figure reduces to a tenth once you are established, by which time a small display advertisement in several local and regional papers to assure shoppers that you are still in business will more than suffice.

One further point on publicity and advertising: your relationship with your traders. Remember that your traders are just as important to your market as your customers. Courtesy costs nothing, and the best traders, those who are running established businesses, will feel much more inclined to support a new market if it is run by an operator who has a good working relationship with, and tries his best to support, his traders.

Appendices

Appendix 1
Useful Organisations

Institute of Market Officers

Formed in 1943 the IMO has the following objectives:

(a) To provide an organisation for market officers and to improve the administration of markets, fairs, abattoirs and cold stores by fostering a knowledge of the work required for their efficient management.
(b) To encourage the study of all questions connected with the administration of markets, abattoirs and allied undertakings under the control of public authorities.
(c) To hold meetings for discussion of matters related to markets administration and for social intercourse between members.
(d) To hold examinations and grant diplomas to members on attaining the required standards.
(e) To carry out any other acts on behalf of the members for the furtherance of the interests and objective of the Institute.

Membership of the Institute is open to persons who are employed by public authorities in the appropriate fields.

It is unlikely that the ordinary market trader will come into contact with the IMO but it is useful to know of its existence as far as general background is concerned, and the mere fact that the Institute exists does show that markets are a substantial and secure section of business generally.

The address is: Institute of Market Officers, Locke Avenue, Barnsley, South Yorkshire S70 1QH; tel 0226 203314.

National Association of British Market Authorities

NABMA was formed in 1948 by the amalgamation of several regional market associations, the earliest of which was founded in 1919.

Membership is open to any local or public authority in Great Britain, Northern Ireland or the Channel Isles having control of public markets, fairs, abattoirs or cold stores.

It has a number of objectives which all have the same aim: to organise local authorities to campaign for and protect their markets and allied businesses. NABMA is vociferous on such matters as changes in legislation etc, and is also keen to promote high standards among market administrators.

The address is: National Association of British Market Authorities, 19 Derwent Avenue, Milnrow, Rochdale, Lancashire OL16 3UD; tel 0706 57740.

National Market Traders' Federation

NMTF is the only organisation which truly represents the individual market trader. It has a strong commitment to protecting its members' interests and a high level of credibility with local authorities in areas where it operates. Branches are organised on a market-by-market basis and most branches are active in member protection and socially. New traders are advised at least to talk to the secretary of the branch on the market nearest to their home or, even better, on the market where they are considering trading.

There is no obligation for a trader to be a member of any trade organisation, and this includes NMTF, but the majority of established traders join and reap the benefits of membership.

A column of Federation news appears each week in the *Market Trader* supplement of *World's Fair* and traders can see from this and from the news reports how active the organisation is.

Various conferences are held in all parts of the country and the Federation can obtain good rates for such things as public liability insurance.

Federation membership is not restricted to any one particular market and a member, say, of the Leicester branch does not need to be a member at any other markets he attends.

NMTF can be contacted at: Hampton House, Hawshaw Lane, Hoyland, Barnsley S77 0HA; tel 0226 749021; fax 0226 740329.

Association of Private Market Operators

This is the newest of the organisations in the markets business. It is made up of a number of private market operators who have banded together to set up an organisation representing the interests of market operators and set minimum standards for their companies by way of a members' Code of Practice.

From the trader's point of view the Association is useful in that it guarantees certain standards on how markets are run and how traders are dealt with. A trader working a market run by an Association member does at least have limited protection, unlike the trader on an independent event.

APMO's address is: c/o The Olde Workhouse, Ducks Hill Road, Ruislip, Middlesex HA4 7TS; tel 0895 675558.

Other useful addresses

Alliance of Small Firms and Self-Employed People
   33 The Green, Calne, Wiltshire SN11 8DJ; tel 0249 817003
British Insurance and Investment Brokers' Association
   14 Bevis Marks, London EC3A 7NT; tel 071-623 9043
Business in the Community
   227A City Road, London EC1V 1LX; tel 071-253 3716
Health and Safety Executive
   Baynard's House, 1 Chepstow Place, Westbourne Grove, London W2 4TF; tel 071-221 0870
HM Customs and Excise
   VAT Administration Directorate, New King's Beam House, 22 Upper Ground, London SE1 9PJ; tel 071-620 1313; also local offices
Scottish Business in the Community
   Romano House, 43 Station Road, Corstorphine, Edinburgh EH12 7AF; tel 031-334 9876

Publications

Market Trader

Market Trader is the only weekly national newspaper for market traders. It is invaluable to the trader, whether he or she is a newcomer or has many years' experience.

It is a supplement of *World's Fair* which is published weekly in Oldham, near Manchester. It is a true national newspaper and is obtainable on subscription from World's Fair Ltd or can be ordered from newsagents.

As a working resource it cannot be bettered and it contains regular advertising for all the new markets opening up and down the country - or at least all those worth attending. Its news columns are fully up to date on all the developments in the market world including new markets and events, changes in legislation, trends and personalities.

Each week there are features on several wholesale warehouses and literally hundreds of warehouses advertise in every possible area of the markets business. From time to time there are supplements with many pages of advertisements featuring the wholesalers in a specific city or region and these can build up into a useful reference file.

Other advertising features stalls and equipment and there is also a regular review of fruit and vegetable markets.

I cannot speak too highly of *World's Fair's* usefulness to the market trader.

Any trader experiencing difficulty obtaining the paper from a newsagent should contact the publisher, World's Fair Ltd, at 2 Daltry Street, Shaw Road, Oldham OL1 4BB; tel 061-624 3687.

The Trader

Another periodical which is useful to traders is *The Trader*, a monthly magazine-type publication from the Link House Advertising Periodicals Group of Poole in Dorset.

Again this is available from most large newsagents or by post from the publisher on a subscription basis. A form for taking out a subscription appears every week in the business section of *Exchange & Mart.*

The Trader places more emphasis on supplies and most of its pages carry advertising from trade wholesale warehouses. There are a few advertisements for markets and events and an increasing amount of editorial coverage but its usefulness is in identifying suppliers of various types of goods.

The publisher's address is: Link House Advertising Periodicals Group, Link House, West Street, Poole, Dorset BH15 1LL; tel 0202 671171.

The Markets Year Book

This is a useful annual publication from the World's Fair publishing group. It gives details of all the established markets in the country, together with information about opening days, operators, market managers etc. It is published in a small paperback format and will fit easily into your glove compartment or briefçase. It is especially useful to the new trader who is trying to establish a run of markets. It includes a directory of wholesalers.

For details contact World's Fair Ltd, 2 Daltry Street, Shaw Road, Oldham OL1 4BB; tel 061-624 3687.

Further reading from Kogan Page

Do Your Own Bookkeeping, Max Pullen
How to Buy a Business, 2nd edition, Peter Farrell
How to Prepare a Business Plan, Edward Blackwell
Law for the Small Business, 7th edition, Patricia Clayton
Starting a Successful Small Business, 2nd edition, M J Morris
Working for Yourself: The Daily Telegraph Guide to Self-Employment, 13th edition, Godfrey Golzen

Some Private Operators

This list is by no means exhaustive and should only be used as a rough guide. Details are given of some of the larger, more established companies. Full lists can be found either in the weekly *World's Fair*, or in *The Markets Year Book*.

Grenchurch Ltd

Grenchurch Ltd operates a large number of mid-week markets in the Cotswolds/Oxfordshire area.

The address is: Grenchurch Ltd, Ganborough Road, Longborough, Moreton in the Marsh, Gloucestershire GL56 0RE; tel 0451 32275; fax 0451 31979.

Wendy Fair

Wendy Fair is a long established company, probably one of the biggest in the country. It is best known for its operation at Finmere in Buckinghamshire which has been in action for over 20 years and has many hundreds of stall units in the season. It is one of the few Sunday market sites with its own purpose-built toilet and catering blocks.

The address is: Wendy Fair, The Olde Workhouse, Ducks Hill Road, Ruislip, Middlesex HA4 7TS; tel 0895 675558.

Graysim Group

This is one of the companies which set up following the repeal of the Sunday Fairs Act in the late 1960s/early 1970s. It has seen some changes since it first opened and now operates a number of mid-week markets, mainly in market halls in various parts of the country.

The address is: Graysim Group, Bowles Farm, Threehouseholds, Chalfont St Giles, Buckinghamshire HP8 4LW; tel 02407 71277.

Bray Associates

Bray Associates is an active company with both open and closed markets in most parts of the country. It is very active in the South East.

Contact tel 0895 639912/0895 637269; fax 0895 622170.

Gramlo

This is a relatively new company but it operates a couple of excellent markets. Its flagship is the Sunday market at Donington Park in Leicestershire and it operates a good market every bank holiday Monday at Melton Mowbray.

Its address is: Gramlo, Kirklington Road, Bilsthorpe, Nottinghamshire; tel 0623 870327/0773 763899.

M & B Markets

M & B Markets operate good bank holiday markets and also organise markets at a number of major outdoor show promotions, particularly in the Midlands.

The address is: M & B Markets, The Manor House, 170–172 Long Street, Atherstone, Warwickshire CV9 1AE; tel 0827 713452.

Midland Markets

Midland Markets operate in South Yorkshire and other areas, all with planning consent on town or village centre sites. All markets are fully legal established events.

The address is: Midland Markets, Hazelwood House, Burmington, Shipston-on-Stour, Warwickshire CV36 5AR; tel 0608 61206.

Sherman & Waterman Associates Ltd

Sherman & Waterman Associates Ltd organise a number of markets in London and the South East.

The address is: Sherman & Waterman Associates Ltd, Freepost WC5379, London WC2E 8BR; tel 071-240 7405.

Leo Promotions

Leo Promotions are particularly active with open markets in the south-east Midlands – mostly mid-week, with occasional forays into Sunday operations.

The address is: Leo Promotions, 12 Main Road, Kilsby, Rugby CV23 8XP; tel 0203 635455/0788 823234.

Index

accountant 32
account books 33, 34
accounts 31
advance rents 21
advertising 77–82
  classified 80
  ongoing 80
  radio and television 80
  shoppers 80
  traders 79
APMO 60, 86
Association of Private Market
  Operators 60, 86

bank accounts 35, 36
barbecues 53
bookkeeping 31
Bray Associates 92
British Market Authorities,
  National Association of 85–6

car boot sales 41–5
cash books 34
cash handling 29
Castle Donington Market 60
casual staff 36
casual traders 20
catering 16, 69–76
  industrial estates 50, 51
  mobile 49–53
  roadside 50
  sites 50
  vans and trailers 52–3
charters 55, 56
checklist (daily) 27
Christmas cards 17
claims, false 28
clothing 14
Consumer Protection Act *1987*
  67–8
counter stalls 25
covered food 71

Day-glo cards 27
demonstrators 15
Department of Transport 51

East of England Show 45
eating areas 69
employee liability insurance 37
employing staff 36
Enterprise Allowance 18
Environmental Health
  Departments 66, 70, 73
European Court 65
Exchange & Mart 52

Finmere Market 59
fire-fighting precautions 75
first aid box 75
fish 18
fishing tackle 14
flea markets 45
flowers 18
fly-posting 58
fly traders 47
Food Act *1984* 69, 70
Food Hygiene (General)
  Regulations *1970* 70
Food Hygiene (Markets, Stalls
  and Delivery Vehicles)
  Regulations *1966* 70
  and Amendment Regulations
  1966 70
food premises 69, 70
Food Safety Act *1990* 70
food, sale of 14, 15
fruit and vegetables 17

gas cylinders 73–5
Gas (Installation and Servicing)
  Regulations *1984* 73
General Development Order
  1963 55
gold 13–14

goods for sale, choice of 13-18
Gramlo 60, 92
Graysim Group 91
Great Yorkshire Show 45
Grenchurch Ltd 91

Halifax Building Society 36
High Court 41, 55
holiday markets 46
hygiene 76

Ingleston Market 59
Inland Revenue 31, 33
Institute of Market Officers 85
insurance 26

law 65
Law of Markets and Fairs 68
Leo Promotions 92
licences (street trading) 47
limited companies 32
Local Government Act 56
LPG (liquified petroleum gas) 73

M & B Markets 92
market halls 40
Market Officers, Institute of 85
market operating 55-60
market research 13, 19
Market Trader 20, 89
Market Traders' Federation,
    National 26, 37, 86
Markets Year Book 20, 63, 90
Midland Markets 92
misleading bargain offers 68
misrepresentation 68
mobile catering 49-53, 69-71
    and see catering
money matters 18

National Association of British
    Market Authorities 85-6
National Market Traders'
    Federation 26, 37, 86
non-charter private markets
    39-40

open foods 70
operating car boot sales 43
outdoor events 23

partnerships 32

pavement artists 48
perishable goods 17
Petticoat Lane, London 23
pirate markets 59
pitching 16
price marking 27
Price Marking (Food) Order *1978*
    69
Price Marking (Food and Drink
    on Premises) Order *1979* 69
pricing 28
Prince's Trust 18
Private Market Operators,
    Association of 60, 86
private markets 39
profits 34, 35
publicity and advertising 77
public liability insurance 26

Quayside Market, Newcastle 23

records, keeping 33
Registrar of Business Names 32
rents and rent collection 22
Royal Show 45

Sale of Goods Act *1979* 67, 69
scales and measuring tools 26
Scottish markets 23, 59
seasonal goods 17
seasonal markets 46
setting up 27-9
Sherman & Waterman Associates
    Ltd 92
Shops Act *1950* 56, 57, 65-6
shows 23, 45
sole trader 32
space, getting a market 19-23, 27
specified goods 20, 21
Spook Erection 59
stall allocation 21
stalls 25
start-up capital 18
steam rallies 45
stock 24-5
stock management 29
street trading 46-8
Sunday Fairs Act 22, 66
Sunday markets 22-3, 40, 57, 66
Sunday trading 57
suppliers 16, 61-4
supply areas 69

taxation 31, 34–5
temperature control 76
theft 28
town markets 39
Trade Descriptions Act *1968* 68
Trader 89–90
Trading Standards Departments 66, 68
transport 23–4

Unfair Contract Terms Act *1977* 67
Useful addresses 85–7

Value Added Tax (VAT) 31, 32, 62

walk-through stalls 25
Warwick City Council 41
weekly planning 20
Wendy Fair 60, 91
Westlers Ltd 53
wholesalers 16, 18
    and see suppliers
World's Fair 20, 78